COME,
LET US
CELEBRATE!

COME, LET US CELEBRATE!

A Resource Book of Contemporary Worship Services

BLAIR RICHARDS &
JANICE SIGMUND

HAWTHORN BOOKS, INC.
W. Clement Stone, *Publisher*
NEW YORK

Library of Congress Catalog Card Number: 75-215
ISBN: 0-8015-1457-6
1 2 3 4 5 6 7 8 9 10

Saying "yes" to Christ and his Church . . .
Finding worship to be true celebration . . .
Having now realized the power of the resurrection . . .

We dedicate this book
to the memory of
our Christian brother,

Louten D. Murray

Contents

Acknowledgments

Bible Version

Quotations from the following versions are used by permission of the copyright holders and are credited in the text with the appropriate abbreviations:

Holy Bible, Revised Standard Version (RSV). New York: Copyright, 1971, National Council of Churches of Christ in the USA.

The Living Bible (LB). Wheaton, Illinois: Copyright, 1972, Tyndale House.

The New English Bible (NEB). New York: Copyright, 1970, Oxford University Press/Cambridge University Press.

The New Testament in Modern English (PT). Translated by J. B. Phillips. New York: Copyright, 1966, Macmillan Publishing Company.

The Psalms for Modern Man (TEV). Translated by the American Bible Society. New York: Copyright, 1970, American Bible Society.

Today's English Version of the New Testament (TEV). Translated by the American Bible Society. New York: Copyright, 1971, 1972, American Bible Society.

Other Sources

Material from *Risk* magazine, published by World Council of Churches, New York, vol. 1, nos. 3 and 4, 1965.

Material from *He Sent Leanness: A Book of Prayers for the Natural Man* by David Head, reprinted by permission of The Macmillan Company. Copyright, 1962, by The Macmillan Company.

Material from *A Diary of Private Prayer* by John Baillie, reprinted by permission of Charles Scribner's Sons. Copyright, 1949, by Charles Scribner's Sons.

Material from *Ventures in Worship 1* edited by David J. Randolph, reprinted by permission of Abingdon Press. Copyright, 1969, by Abingdon Press.

Material from *Call to Commitment* by Elizabeth O'Connor, reprinted by permission of Harper & Row. Copyright, 1963, by Harper & Row.

Material from *Ventures in Worship 3* edited by David J. Randolph, reprinted by permission of Abingdon Press. Copyright, 1970, by Abingdon Press.

Material from *The Good Friday Service of Tenebrae* by Charles E. Ferrell, paraphrased by permission of C.S.S. Publishing Co. Copyright, 1971, by C.S.S. Publishing Co.

Material from *Interrobang* by Norman C. Habel, reprinted by permission of Fortress Press. Copyright, 1969, by Fortress Press.

"Communion Liturgy" reprinted by permission of United University Church, 331 Seventeenth Avenue, SE, Minneapolis, Minnesota 55414.

Voices by Oscar J. Rumpf, reprinted from *Cries from the Hurting Edge of the World*. Copyright, 1970, by Oscar J. Rumpf. Used by permission of John Knox Press, Atlanta, Georgia.

And They Came to See by Charles and Mary Walker, 2309 Bell St., Columbus, Georgia 31906. Reprinted by permission of the authors.

Material from *Ventures in Worship 2* edited by David J. Randolph, reprinted by permission of Abingdon Press. Copyright, 1970, by Abingdon Press.

Material from *Hymns Hot and Carols Cool* by Richard Avery and Donald Marsh, reprinted by permission of Proclamation Productions, Inc. Copyright, n.d., by Proclamation Productions, Inc.

Material from *Creative Brooding* by Robert A. Raines, reprinted by permission of The Macmillan Company. Copyright, 1966, by The Macmillan Company.

Material from *Reshaping the Christian Life* by Robert A. Raines, reprinted by permission of Harper & Row. Copyright, 1964, by Harper & Row.

Material from *God Is No Fool* by Lois Cheney, reprinted by permission of Abingdon Press. Copyright, 1969, by Abingdon Press.

Material from *Christian Clippings*, reprinted by permission of *Christian Clippings*. Copyright, November, 1972, by *Christian Clippings*.

Material from *Worship Pac*, issues 14, 15, 17, edited by Wesley D. Taylor, reprinted by permission of Center for Worship Reformation, Inc. Copyright, May, July, October, 1973, by Center for Worship Reformation, Inc.

"Prayer for MIAs" by Richard D'Arcy. Copyright VIVA (Vital Voices of America), Los Angeles, California.

Material from *Catch the New Wind* by Marilee Zdenek and Marge Champion, reprinted by permission of Word Books. Copyright, 1972, by Word Books.

Material from *In the Stillness Is the Dancing* by Mark Link, reprinted by permission of Argus Communications. Copyright, 1972, by Argus Communications.

Material from *Take Off Your Shoes* by Mark Link, reprinted by permission of Argus Communications. Copyright, 1972, by Argus Communications.

Material from *Tell It Like It Is* by Ralph Carmichael and Kurt Kaiser, reprinted by permission of Lexicon Music, Inc. Copyright, 1969, by Lexicon Music, Inc.

Material from poster "I'm So Glad That You Are Here" by M. Rilke, reprinted by permission of Argus Communications. Copyright, ca. 1970, by Argus Communications.

Material from *Journey Inward—Journey Outward* by Elizabeth O'Connor, reprinted by permission of Harper & Row. Copyright, 1968, by Harper & Row.

Material from *Folk Dancing* by Richard G. Kraus, reprinted by permission of The Macmillan Company. Copyright, 1962, by The Macmillan Company.

Material from *Words Are No Good if the Game Is Solitaire* by Herbert B. Barks, Jr., reprinted by permission of Word Books, Inc. Copyright, 1971, by Word Books, Inc.

Material from *Act One* by Moss Hart reprinted by permission of Random House, Inc. Copyright 1959 by Catherine Carlisle and Joseph Hyman, trustees.

Material from *The Confessions of St. Augustine*, translated by F. J. Sheed. Copyright 1943. Used by permission of Sheed and Ward, Inc.

"The Oxen" from *The Collected Poems of Thomas Hardy*. Copyright 1925 by The Macmillan Co., Inc. Reprinted by permission of the Hardy Estate; Macmillan London & Basingstroke and The Macmillan Company of Canada.

Material from *Celebration* by Clarence Rivers. Copyright 1969 by Clarence Joseph Rivers. Used by permission of the publisher, Seabury Press, Inc.

I
PROLOGUE

Credos and Credits

Contemporary worship, worship celebration, new forms of worship; all these are terms for something that's new, different, and exciting—a way of making worship come alive in today's Christian community. Yet there are practical struggles involved in putting together these exciting and current services.

This book is our attempt to share the trials and tribulations, the joys and celebrations, the sometimes painful growth involved in creating a program of meaningful worship. In our search, we found few really practical sources of help. So we decided to write this book as an aid for all who search with us.

Come, Let Us Celebrate! begins with an account of why and how our new forms of worship were initiated. It then shares the steps we took, the preparation we made, and the growth we are experiencing now. In Part II you are invited to sample some services. This is designed to provide suggestions to use complete or as points of beginning. We hope that these services will help you to begin . . . to be unafraid . . . to let go while the Holy Spirit soars.

We thank the many people who encouraged us to write this book. Special thanks to our families, especially to Jim Sigmund, whose support, enthusiasm, and encouragement have been most valuable; and to Troy Richards, whose six years of age inspire hope and new life in the church of the future. Friends and supporters who attend these worship services contributed greatly —especially our guitarists, Melinda Carpenter, Doug McFarland, and Sharon Pederson. We are indebted to our church's associate pastor, Rev. William Greer; to its director of music, H. E. McFarland; to our willing implementor, Norris Randall; and to our friend and typist, John Miller.

A multitude of exciting people who already know the joys and struggles of celebrating influenced us. These people include Thom Jones, Nashville, Tennessee; Dennis Benson, Pittsburgh, Pennsylvania; Lyman Coleman, Scottdale, Pennsylvania; Dan Kennedy, Goleta, California; Jim Strathdee, San Pedro, California; and John Atwood, San Diego, California. Many others shared with us through their writings, including: Mark Link, James White, Ross Snyder, Robert Raines, and Elizabeth O'Connor.

Bless them all!

Begin, Began, Begun

Do you need more meaningful worship experience?

Do you feel a sameness as you follow the basic order of service week after week?

Do you feel that you worship just as your ancestors did?

Do you need to break free and say, "Hooray, God!"?

Such questions focused on our need to praise, adore, give thanks—to worship in a contemporary way. As we began to talk about the need for a fresh wind in our worship, other people started to join in. For many of us, traditional worship had lost its spark.

Not that we wanted to do away with the traditional. After all, traditional forms of worship continue to be meaningful to many people. But we were convinced that new life was waiting to be set free through new worship forms. The pace of our technological age and all that it entails opened wider visions for celebrations for coming alive for the Lord, for clapping hands and shouting for joy.

> What is Celebration?
>
> Celebration is re-living and re-tasting memorable experiences where the meaning of life breaks through, and we say to these events, "Remain with me. Be me."
>
> Celebration is a people of setting out through time toward a destiny, with their treasures of memories and meanings.
>
> What is Celebration? It is entering into the creating and redeeming which is now making mankind.
>
> And participating in such transactions with a certain amount of reckless abandon. It is a mode of being in the world; pervaded and held together by an ocean of feeling which reports tremendous and fascinating mystery. We know that we are dealing with The Holy. We are hilariously turned in to God and fellow man.
>
> (*Risk* Magazine)

Our own worship celebration is now one-and-a-half years old. Creating, assembling, planning, and executing our services are deep personal experiences, and we look back with enthusiasm at the many themes, approaches, and people that have been involved.

Indeed, to us the celebration of worship *is* involvement—involvement in and through every area, event, talent, and feeling that life offers. We see worship as a gathering together in order that when we scatter we may become living Christs where we are.

Yet starting such a celebration was far from easy. While many people agreed that new forms of worship were needed, many others feared the suggested changes. With hopes for official sanction dimming, a small group set aside time to pray and to fast—to let God take control.

And something beautiful happened. The leaders and officials on our church's governing council and board granted our request for an eight-week trial period. Our worship celebrations would be directed through the education program and were set for 8:30 each Sunday morning. An evaluation would follow the proposed trial period.

These eight initial services included as many new formats as possible: a parade, a first-person sermon, a dialogue sermon, the building of heaven machines, graffiti, a lot of music (folk, traditional, contemporary, classical), role-plays, a play written and produced by eighth-graders, large- and small-group discussions, and various forms of communion, creeds, prayers, and litanies.

Having no idea how our community of worshipers would respond to this varied fare, we learned many valuable lessons—especially that people are willing to try to worship in unfamiliar ways. Our orders of service almost always looked good on paper, sounded good as we read through them, and felt good as we planned and rehearsed. But until we experienced these services with our worship community, we could not know how worshipful these new forms actually were. Seeing our community come alive in worship was wonderful. Some of our attempts did fail—but all the worship celebrations, including the failures, created enthusiasm that spilled out beyond the bounds of our worship settings.

Our initial eight services received such a positive evaluation from our church board that we were granted approval for new-form services to be held on a regular weekly basis beginning that fall. This approval was unanimous. We knew that God was with us, and our gratitude showed in our lives.

Since you are reading this book of shared thoughts and plans, perhaps you already are interested or involved in leading worship. Through our experience, we encourage you to be enablers rather than leaders, to help others use their gifts and talents—big or small, seen or unseen. Everyone has a gift that can be channeled into a significant, meaningful, fulfilling role in celebrating worship. It is essential to release the gifts of each participant. To be free to be oneself, to give, to take, to be—that is worship. To be aware, totally aware, of one's total being—that is celebration!

Another basic point is that our services are grounded in Scripture. As we bring together all that is necessary for worship each week, our own feelings are grounded in the fulfillment of Scripture. Worshiping together, we encounter God as a community of believers. We celebrate worship in response to the victory that must be shared. Worship is the celebration of life in Christ, and it is central to our Christian faith.

"Jehovah is our God, Jehovah alone. You must love him with all your heart, soul and might" (Deut. 6:4, The Living Bible). We believe these words and find in them the foundation of our worship. As the psalm says:

> Sing for joy to the Lord, all the world!
> Worship the Lord gladly,
> and come before him with joyful songs!
>
> Never forget that the Lord is God!
>   He made us, and we belong to him;
>   we are his people, we are his flock.
>
> Enter his temple with thanksgiving,
>   go into his sanctuary with praise!
>   Give thanks to him and praise him!
>
> The Lord is good;
>   his love lasts forever,
>   and his faithfulness for all time.
>
> (Ps. 100, TEV)

Then we read the all-important words in Matt. 28: 1–6 (TEV):

After the Sabbath, as Sunday morning was dawning, Mary Magdalene and the other Mary went to look at the grave. Suddenly there was a strong earthquake; an angel of the Lord came down from heaven, rolled the stone away, and sat on it. His appearance was like lightning and his clothes white as snow. The guards were so afraid that they trembled and became like dead men.

The angel spoke to the women. "You must not be afraid," he said. "I know you are looking for Jesus who was nailed to the cross. He is not here; he has risen, just as he said."

The victory of Christ is for each of us. This central point in our Christian faith is where we need to begin—and where you, too, must begin. So join us and celebrate! Celebrate the victory we have in Jesus Christ! Now is the time. Hooray!

Before getting deeply involved with specific service ideas and plans, roll up your sleeves and take a few minutes now to think things through. A great deal of thought, work, and prayer must be done before you can actually begin new-form services.

When you have the answers to the following questions firmly set in your mind, you should be ready to implement the service ideas presented in Part II.

How Will the Week-after-Week Work Get Done?

Our organization hinges on a volunteer coordinator who understands worship, organizes programs and people well, and willingly spends much time in research. This coordinator of new-form worship services is responsible to one of the boards of our church. Letting this coordinator be part of your worship and/or education structure provides a tie-in with the ongoing local church.

Our coordinator works closely with our pastor and directors of education and music. The innovations in worship produced by this team effort are not construed as opposing the more traditional worship forms.

Choosing the right coordinator is probably the most important factor in setting up this type of organizational structure. But even after your coordinator has been chosen and approved, your task has just begun.

You must make the basic decision of how you will implement your worship innovations. Will you develop a completely separate service using all new designs? Or will you integrate your innovations into the established worship service?

This book is basically designed for separate services of new-form worship. But we feel that the innovations should be gradually worked into the established services.

Once you've made this decision, the coordinator must begin to gather ideas from every source available. Consider themes for each Sunday. Re-examine the church calendar, look for a Christian angle in national holidays, find out the special concerns of your people and research them, and be sensitive to themes suggested by the Christian faith itself.

As you use this book you will see a variety of sources come alive with ideas. Our techniques, models, settings, and vehicles for carrying out themes are gathered from books, television, and various other media as well as from life experiences.

Sometimes ideas are implemented immediately, but many are mentally shelved until they mature from a seed idea into a workable plan. Ideas should be recorded in a file and kept for the weeks, months, or even longer periods necessary for their maturation.

But Where Do Ideas Originate?
And Where Do You Find Materials about Them?

Listening and reading are two methods for finding valuable ideas. Listen to what your people have to say—their problems, prayers, talents, hopes, and dreams should provide you with many ideas and much meaningful material.

As for reading and book research, we have included a bibliography and resource list at the end of this book, which may serve as a starting point—not only for ideas, but also for a resource collection.

Accumulating all these resources may be financially impossible, but remember to use your church library, public and college libraries, and the libraries of other churches in your community. Denominational offices often lend books, records, films, filmstrips, and other materials.

Compile a list of useful books and their costs. Distribute this list to your membership. Ask for volunteer donations. Perhaps some people will purchase books as memorials or in honor of someone. Bookplates commemorating the honoree may be inserted in the front of these books before they are placed in your church library or special worship library.

You will discover, just as we did, that the world is your source. Human and material resources abound if you look for them. You are limited only by your willingness to search. Finding and using the resources of your community can be a challenge full of fun.

How Do You Pay Your Expenses?

Much of what we do is done with little or no cost. People—even outsiders—are often willing to donate resources, supplies, time, or know-how for new-form services. Remember to use all the resources available in your community. A little work can uncover sources that are free or available at a nominal cost. Our biggest expense has been for books and films.

We began without a funding source, but we found that some financial assistance was necessary. Our church now includes an item for new-form worship services in the budget. After two years of these services, our current budget request is $250.

An offering should be taken up during each service, but we recommend that such income be part of the total church budget and not kept for new-form service funding.

If you are just introducing the concept of new-form services in your congregation, you may want to find a benefactor for your project. An individual or group may provide a sum of money to get you started. This sum should be placed in the church's general budget and earmarked for your purposes.

On Such a Limited Budget, How Do You Promote
the Many Happenings of the New-Form Services?

If you establish a separate new-form service, you must inform the membership about it. At periodic intervals—perhaps yearly—tell them again what, where, when, why, and how.

If you have new-form services on a regular basis, try weekly announcements in the bulletin or newsletter, and ask your minister to mention them when he talks to the membership about worship.

Your best promotion will come from those who participate. Word of mouth is sure to bring response. Point out the importance of sharing to your people. Ask them to tell their friends about new-form services.

Many churches use local newspapers to announce services each Saturday. Be sure that new-form services are included. And be sure that the religion or church editor is aware of them—he may want to do a feature sometime.

Is New-Form Worship More Visual
than Traditional Services?

Visual aids are valuable assets to any service. We try to coordinate them with weekly themes. Visual aids can be almost anything—pictures, posters, banners, boxes, collages, candles, balloons, crosses, worship centers, signs, stones, pieces of yarn. They can be made from anything you have at hand.

Round up old newspapers, magazines, scraps of this and that, markers, and so on. Effective collages can be developed on almost any subject.

We have found it meaningful to make banners to express our Christian faith. Gather an intergenerational group and provide them with supplies: burlap, felt, idea books, idea starter items, glue, scissors, etc. It's great fun— and it can provide a creative opportunity for expressing the faith and a common ground for a mixed age group.

How Does Music Fit into a New Form?

Listening and singing provide common elements for all worshipers. Use all types of music: classical, gospel, folk, rock. Every piece of music should be chosen for its aesthetic value and for what it says.

Develop a core of songs that are familiar to worshipers. Repeat songs often, so that people learn them; but do not be afraid to try new songs.

Look for easily singable songs, those that can be sung by any worshiper. To introduce a new song, ask the song leader and musicians to sing and play it as special music one week. Another time, your group might use some pre-service time to learn a new song. Once your group is acquainted with a song, include it in your services for several weeks.

We have, at times, used more than one new song per service. This should be done carefully. The preservice time is best used to learn songs in this case.

The music you choose is important, but your song leader and musicians are equally important. Any musical instrument can be used so reach out to your worshipers and use their talents. We use guitars most often, but we have used piano, drums, trumpets, and flute.

Musicians must rehearse before the service in order to be familiar with the selections to be used. The song leader should work with them; a leader's enthusiasm is most important in leading any song.

In using recorded and taped music, someone should rehearse starting and stopping the tape or record and check the quality of the player and the tape or record prior to the service. Preplanning is a must.

Do New-Form Services Call for New Kinds of Rooms and Room Setups?

Flexibility is a key for us. We are aware, however, that a separate room with no permanent chairs might not be available in all churches. In this case, you can use a sanctuary with permanently fastened pews. Simply adapt the services to the facilities.

And change your space according to the needs of your service. A nature theme might find you worshiping outdoors, for instance. A message calling for a small, confined area might be conducted in the chancel and choir loft. Space is important only in that you learn to adapt what's available to your needs.

In a social hall, fellowship hall, or large classroom, you will have great freedom in room arrangement. We rearrange our seating weekly. This freedom of movement has been beneficial to the total worship experience.

Definitions

Now that we've shared our answers for some of the questions that you may have, we'd like to define some of the methods and terms we use in the service samples that follow. Take a minute to read these explanations in order to avoid confusion as you approach the services.

LEADER OR HOST FAMILY: An individual or a family serving as greeters and leaders for the service. They may do readings, lead in prayer, etc. The experience gives these people a chance to participate. It also gives them an opportunity for developing leadership and growing in the worship experience.

Offering and Community Concerns and Interest: An informal time in our worship, usually led by the host family or leader.

Offerings can take the form of money or self-giving. Both forms are encouraged in our congregation. Since our setting does not require ushers, the leader or host family is in charge of passing a basket or plate and carrying it up to the worship center.

An *offertory prayer* can be given by the leader, host family, or entire worship community. This prayer may be silent or spoken.

The *community concerns and interests* portion of our service is an informal sharing time focusing on community, national, and global concerns. We also use this time for sharing prayer requests, special needs, and hospital lists. Lighter events such as birthdays, births, and honors are also included in this time of awareness in a caring community. Be open of unexpected requests. Be free to speak with worshipers in an informal manner.

Some General Notes

We prepared most services in bulletin form, as shown in this book. In a few cases we limited distribution to people who had leadership roles; in most cases, bulletins were distributed to all worshipers.

Most participants prepare themselves ahead of time and then read their parts. If you feel that a reading would be more effective memorized, do it that way. In the services we've included, we recommend memorization where we feel the need for it.

We call rehearsals only occasionally. But many services need careful coordination; and if a rehearsal would aid the flow of the service, by all means call one.

Knowing Where Your People Are: It is important to be certain where the members of your congregation stand in their spiritual development and in their understanding of mission. In developing services, planners should keep in mind the feelings, attitudes, and awareness of members. If you are considering innovations in worship, you may already have a feel for where your people are. If not, set up some informal small-group meetings to share feelings on worship as well as the mission of the church, the Christian faith, and so on. From these meetings you should be able to draw some valuable conclusions as to "where your people are."

II
CELEBRATIONS

1

Commitment? Recommitment?
(New Years)

IDEA GERM

Today begins a new year of pain and healing, when we begin to try to be brutally honest in reexamining our commitments to Christ. Now is the time to thank God for calling us to be his people.

DESCRIPTION
OF SERVICE

A time of self-examination which is guided by a collection of pertinent readings—even the sermon is a reading. The climax comes as the congregation itself reads silently, then orally, and finally signs commitment statements which are collected to be given out again at the beginning of Lent.

PREPARATION
CHECKLIST

Recruit seven readers and one leader (for benediction), and see that each has his part.

Contact person to deliver Peter Marshall's sermon.

Arrange for a host family.

Inform musicians of songs to rehearse.

Arrange for a soloist or small ensemble to share the special music.

See that the list of commitments is reproduced.

Assemble these lists with envelopes and pencils.

See that the bulletin is designed and reproduced.

Decide how the room should be arranged. This service has no special requirements other than to encourage community among worshipers.

Service Script: Commitment? Recommitment?

PRESERVICE
THOUGHT

Today is a time of pain and healing when we begin to try to be brutally honest in reexamining our commitments to Christ. Now is the time to thank God for calling us to be his people.

CALL TO
WORSHIP

"Be Still" (song by Avery and Marsh)

LOOKING BACK

Reader 1: There was nothing I could reply when you called me: "Rise, thou that sleepest and arise from the dead: and Christ shall enlighten thee"; and whereas you showed me by every evidence that your words were true, there was simply nothing I could answer save only laggard lazy words:
Soon,
Quite soon,
Give me just a little while.
But "soon" and "quite soon" did not mean any particular time; and "just a little while" went on for quite a long while.

(*St. Augustine's* Confessions, *translated by F. J. Sheed*)

Reader 2: St. Matthew stated:

(*Read Matt. 4:18–22, Matt. 9:9, TEV*)

Reader 3: John Wesley declared: "He is secure because he is utterly ignorant of himself. Hence he talks of 'repenting by and by'; he does not indeed exactly know when, but some time or other before he dies; taking it for granted that this is quite in his own power."

(*from John Wesley's sermon "The Spirit of Bondage and of Adoption" as quoted in* He Sent Leanness, Head, *p. 34, fn.*)

Reader 4: Jesus said:

(*Read Matt. 24:36–44, TEV*)

Reader 5: And man prays: O Lord, so long as the
weather is reasonably fine,
so long as I have no visitors,
so long as nobody asks me to do any work,
so long as I can sit in the back pew but one on the left,

so long as it isn't a local preacher planned,
so long as they don't choose hymns I don't know,
so long as my Joe is asked to recite at the Anniversary,
so long as I can get home in time for the play,
I will honour Thee with my presence at Church whenever
I feel like it.

("*Prayers of pious intention*" #4, He Sent Leanness,
Head, *p. 36*)

Reader 6: Jesus said:

(*Read Matt. 22:36–40, TEV*)

LOOKING
INWARD
(*All read in silence; reflect in silence*)

O Merciful Father, who dost look down upon the weaknesses
of Thy human children more in pity than in anger, and more in
love than in pity, let me now in Thy holy presence inquire into
the secrets of my heart.

Have I in the past year done anything to fulfill the purpose for
which Thou didst cause me to be born?

Have I accepted such opportunities of service as Thou in Thy
wisdom hast set before my feet?

Have I performed without omission the plain duties of the day?
  Give me grace to answer honestly, O God.

Have I done anything to tarnish my Christian ideal of life?

Have I been lazy in body or languid in spirit?

Have I wrongfully indulged my bodily appetites?

Have I kept my imagination pure and healthy?

Have I been scrupulously honorable in all my business dealings?

Have I been transparently sincere in all I have professed to be,
to feel, or to do?
  Give me grace to answer honestly, O God.

Have I tried to see myself as others see me?

Have I made more excuses for myself than I have been willing to make for others?

Have I, in my own home, been a peace-maker or have I stirred up strife?

Have I, while professing noble sentiments for great causes and distant objects, failed even in common charity and courtesy towards those nearest to me?
Give me grace to answer honestly, O God.

(A Diary of Private Prayer, *Baillie, p. 43*)

(All read aloud)

God our Father, we have run away from home again, and now we are just wandering around in life. We got carried away by imagination—all those big dreams looked so real and felt so good. But now we know that we are in trouble. We even forgot to do the obvious good things and ended up doing the very things we wanted to avoid. God, give us another chance. For the sake of Jesus Christ, help us to give ourselves to you so that a wonderful, adventurous, sober, good life will be ours. The credit all goes to you. Amen.

(Prayer of Confession by Delton Krueger in Ventures in Worship 1, *edited by Randolph, p. 17)*

LOOKING UPWARD

All: O God, in whose eternal wisdom alone is comprehended the mystery of Time, we thank Thee for the Past because Thou hast forgiven it: we thank Thee for the Future because Thou hast hidden it: we thank Thee for the Present because Thou art wholly present in it, to meet us with Thy creative, redemptive and sanctifying power, if we will awake from all dreams of past and future to live in Thy instant reality. Amen.

(A prayer by Gerald Heard in Leaves from My Spiritual Notebook, *Kepler)*

SPECIAL MUSIC   "Pilgrim Song" (*Joy Is Like the Rain* collection)

Offering, Prayers, Community Concerns and Interests

(Commitment lists and envelopes are distributed as the offering is given. The people are asked to consider these points of commitment, to check the ones they can and to sign their commitment. Each person is further asked to seal his commitment in an envelope with his name on the front. Commitments are taken up, but will be given back for reevaluation the first Sunday in Lent.)

We covenant with Christ and one another to:
Meet God daily in a set time of prayer
Let God confront us daily through the Scriptures
Grow in love for the brotherhood and all people, remembering
    the command, "Love one another as I have loved you."
Worship weekly—normally with our church
Be a vital contributing member of one of the groups
Give proportionately, beginning at a tithe of our incomes
Confess and ask the help of our fellowship should we fail in
    these expressions of devotion.

> *(List of commitments from the minimum discipline of the Church of the Savior, Washington, D.C., from* Call to Commitment, *O'Connor, p. 34)*

LOOKING
AROUND

(Speaker delivers sermon "Dawn Came Too Late" from John Doe, Disciple *by Peter Marshall.)*

LOOKING
AHEAD

Reader 7: Hold fast to God and he will add every good thing. Seek God and you shall find him and all good with him. To the man who cleaves to God, God cleaves and adds virtue. Thus, what you have sought before, now seeks you; what you once pursued, now pursues you; what you once fled, now flees you. Everything comes to him who truly comes to God, bringing all divinity with it, while all that is strange and alien flies away.

> *(by Meister Eckhart in* Leaves from My Spiritual Notebook, *Kepler)*

SINGING "Kum Ba Yah"

> *(Songbook for Saints and Sinners, Young, p. 19)*

BENEDICTION

Leader: The Lord has showed you, O man, what is good; and what does He require of you but to do justice and steadfast love and to walk humbly with your God?
—He is with you as you go forth . . .

(by *Kathryn Rogers Deering in* Ventures in Worship 3, *edited by Randolph, p. 147, #158)*

Reflections

We decided to dramatize the sermon by asking an actor from our local theater group to deliver Peter Marshall's words. Our actor was extremely effective and unusually moving, but Marshall's sermon certainly could be delivered by a minister who doesn't mind using someone else's words.

Readers must be very familiar with their materials; this whole service depends on effective reading.

The host family may set up the room, distribute bulletins, collect offering, and make worshipers feel at home.

2
This Passover Meal
(Lent)

IDEA GERM

To experience the Last Supper as intensely as possible. To be at that Passover feast with the Lord, to be there among his followers, and perhaps to discover new meaning in Holy Communion.

DESCRIPTION
OF SERVICE

The congregation is the added guest while Jesus and his disciples celebrate the last Passover feast before the Crucifixion and Resurrection. Having participated in the hand or foot washing and in the feasting, the congregation listens as the drama of the Last Supper is reenacted, and it partakes of the Communion along with the disciples.

PREPARATION
CHECKLIST

Decide on the menu—which items to use and how much of each. *Note:* Help from a Jewish friend was invaluable for recipes and background materials used at the synagogue. We chose to use matzo (unleavened bread), lamb, charoset (a mixture of apples, nuts, cinnamon, and wine), parsley and salt water, bitter herbs (horseradish), and wine (in our case, grape juice—which is also used for Jewish children).

Arrange for food preparation.

Gather small, plain paper plates, napkins, and cups, and an antique-looking goblet and plate to use as the cup of Elijah and the ceremonial plate. *Note:* We used paper products because we didn't have enough authentic tableware for our large number of people. However, we did use the antiques for the cup of Elijah and the ceremonial plate.

Collect candles. We used seven-branch candelabras at either end of the Lord's table, plus enough other candles for the light needed.

Select persons from your worship community who are comfortable with touching experiences to wash the hands or feet of your congregation.

Procure a bowl or bowls, and towels for hand or foot washing.

Recruit a good reader, twelve disciples, and your minister (to portray Christ).

Decide on tables, table coverings, room arrangements, and seating methods. *Note:* We arranged our tables in a rectangle, the width determined by the space needed to seat thirteen men, the sides and other end determined by the number we expected. The opposite end of the Lord's table was left with an opening to facilitate any extra serving that might be needed. For a large group, place bowls and towels at several entrances. For small congregations, up to fifty, one entry way will be enough.

Acquire record player and record or tape player and tape of Lenten selections from the *Messiah.* Place equipment away from the tables so that the music is heard only faintly.

Develop a bulletin to list, describe, and symbolize the foods. Explanations of the cup of Elijah and the Passover feast should also be included.

Service Script: This Passover Meal

EXPLANATION

Pesach or Passover is so called because God "passed over the houses of the people of Israel in Egypt when he slew the Egyptians" (Exod. 12:27, TEV) and liberated the Hebrew people held captive in Goshen.

ENTER

(As people enter the worship room, their hands or feet are washed by selected members of the worship community who are comfortable while touching others. After the washing, they seat themselves at tables which are set with Passover foods. They may refer to their programs for the following information.)

SYMBOLS

Matzo—unleavened bread in the form of large crackers, symbol of the slaves' affliction in Egypt and a reminder of their hasty departure.

A roasted shankbone—symbol of the paschal sacrifice which our ancestors brought to the Temple. (We used roasted lamb.)

Bitter herbs—symbol of the bitterness of Israel's bondage in Egypt. (We used horseradish.)

A roasted egg—symbol of sacrifices brought to the Temple on festive occasions.

Charoset—a mixture of apples, nuts, cinnamon, and wine—symbol of the mortar used by the Hebrews to build the "treasure cities of Pharaoh."

Parsley, lettuce, watercress (or any other green herb), plus a dish of salt water—symbol of spring's coming, suggesting the perpetual renewal of life and, hence, the ever-sustaining hope of human redemption. (We used parsley and salt water.)

Wine—symbol of God's promise of redemption to Israel: "I will bring you out . . . I will deliver you . . . I will redeem you . . . I will take you . . ." (Exod. 6:6–7). (We used grape juice.)

Salt water—symbol of the tears shed in Egypt.

Cup of Elijah—symbol of Elijah, who has always been associated with the coming of the Messiah. (Placed on the disciples' feast table.)

FEAST

Informal table conversations and feasting occur for about fifteen minutes. Background music from the *Messiah* plays during this interval.

SCRIPTURE
REFERENCE

John 13 and 14, Luke 22:14–20

SCRIPT

(All Scripture in this service is from TEV)

Reader: It was now the day before the feast of Passover. Jesus knew that his hour had come for him to leave this world and go to the Father. He had always loved those who were his own in the world, and he loved them to the very end.

(John 13:1)

(Reader gives cue to each disciple prior to their words, e.g., "Simon, do you wish to speak?")

Simon the Zealot: I am Simon. As a member of the Zealots, the Jewish patriots conspiring to ignite a revolution against Rome, I found Jesus' noninvolvement in our movement hard to accept. But I took time to listen to him, to live with him, to follow. Now I understand that love is the only way to deal with the force and power in the world.

(Jesus makes spontaneous remarks to Simon.)

Reader: Jesus and his disciples were at supper. The devil had already decided that Judas, the son of Simon Iscariot, would betray Jesus. Jesus knew that the Father had given him complete power; he knew that he had come from God and was going to God. So Jesus rose from the table, took off his outer garment, and tied a towel around his waist. Then he poured some water into a washbasin and began to wash the disciples' feet and dry them with the towel around his waist. He came to Simon Peter, who said to him, "Are you going to wash my feet, Lord?" Jesus answered him, "You do not know now what I am doing, but you will know later." Peter declared, "You will never, at any time, wash my feet!" "If I do not wash your feet," Jesus answered, "you will no longer be my disciple." Simon Peter answered, "Lord, do not wash only my feet, then! Wash my hands and head, too!"

(John 13:2–9)

Peter: Quick-tempered, impulsive, overconfident—that's bound to be me: Peter! I like to talk and have a knack for making my own troubles. Yet I was perceptive enough to know Jesus as the Messiah while he was still with us. After asking too many questions, I came up with the right answer.

Jesus saw the stuff of a natural church leader somewhere in me and encouraged me as I made my rough-and-tumble way to faith. Yes, I'm very sorry that I denied our Lord, but I'm sure he continued to have faith in me even then. He believes in all of us—even when we don't!

(Jesus makes spontaneous remarks to Peter.)

Reader: Jesus said: "Whoever has taken a bath is completely clean and does not have to wash himself, except for his feet. All of you are clean—except one." Jesus already knew who was going to betray him; that is why he said, "All of you, except one, are clean."

After he had washed their feet, Jesus put his outer garment back on and returned to his place at the table. "Do you understand what I have just done to you?" he asked. "You call me Teacher and Lord, and it is right that you do so, because I am. I am your Lord and Teacher, and I have just washed your feet. You, then, should wash each other's feet. I have set an example for you, so that you will do just what I have done for you."

(John 13:10–15)

James:	My name is James. My brother, John, and I were two of Jesus' closest friends, although many people would tell you that Jesus and I have little in common. Their accusations that I am ambitious, temperamental, and power-seeking are true. Yet Jesus saw that even I could be guided to be a creative and valuable servant. Now his purpose is my purpose; his mission, my mission.

(Jesus makes spontaneous remarks to James.)

Reader:	I tell you the truth: no slave is greater than his master; no messenger is greater than the one who sent him. Now you know this truth; how happy you will be if you put it into practice!

(John 13:16–17)

James, the son of Alphaeus:	Although my feelings were anti-Roman, I was nonviolent in my opposition. I am James, the son of Alphaeus and a relative of Matthew. In spite of our kinship, Matthew and I usually were on opposite sides no matter what the issue—until Jesus came along. He was able to unite us in work for a common cause: his kingdom. His reconciling love can guide diverse people and factions into Christian cooperation.

(Jesus makes spontaneous remarks to this James.)

Reader:	"I am not talking about all of you; I know those I have chosen. But the scripture must come true that says, 'The man who ate my food turned against me.' I tell you this now before it hap-

pens, so that when it does happen you will believe that 'I Am Who I Am.' I tell you the truth; whoever receives anyone I send, receives me also; and whoever receives me, receives him who sent me."

(John 13:18–20)

Andrew: People know me as an outgoing fisherman. I am Peter's brother, Andrew. One of my favorite pastimes is getting to know people and helping them to know one another, but I enjoy helping people to know the Lord most of all. I'm delighted to tell you that I introduced Peter to Jesus as well as being the first to bring non-Jews to meet our Lord. And, yes, I invited the boy with the loaves and fish to come to see Jesus. Christ made me the way I am. He uses me to reach out to men and bring them to him. Praise the Lord!

(Jesus makes spontaneous remarks to Andrew.)

Reader: After Jesus said this, he was deeply troubled, and declared openly: "I tell you the truth: one of you is going to betray me." The disciples looked at one another, completely puzzled about whom he meant. One of the disciples, whom Jesus loved, was sitting next to Jesus.

(John 13:21–23)

John: You've already met my brother James, but now it's my turn—I'm John. Some people have dubbed me a son of thunder, since I'm quick to shake my fist at people who are unresponsive to Jesus and his message. I've also been known to stop a stranger who was healing in the name of my Lord. In spite of my intolerances, however, I always remain close to Christ. He even called me "the beloved disciple" once, making me come to know how his love has changed this "son of thunder." My intolerant nature has become a channel for his love. Such a change can happen to anyone who lets Jesus take charge.

(Jesus makes spontaneous remarks to John.)

Reader: Simon Peter motioned to him and said, "Ask him who it is that he is talking about." So that disciple moved closer to Jesus' side and asked, "Who is it, Lord?" Jesus answered, "I will dip the bread in the sauce and give it to him; he is the man." So he took a piece of bread, dipped it, and gave it to Judas, the son of Simon Iscariot. As soon as Judas took the bread, Satan went into him. Jesus said to him, "Hurry and do what you must!"

None of those at the table understood what Jesus said to him. Since Judas was in charge of the moneybag, some of the disciples thought that Jesus had told him to go to buy what they needed for the feast, or else that he had told him to give something to the poor.

Judas accepted the bread and went out at once. It was night.

(John 13:24–30)

Judas: You know me well: I am Judas, the treasurer of the twelve—and, yes, the betrayer. Some people might tell you that I was a revolutionary who longed for the Roman rulers to be dethroned at any price. Since Jesus remained aloof from my plots and schemes, I thought I could goad him into action by betraying him to the very authorities I was sure we both hated. But my calculations were all miscalculations, rendering my Lord crucified because of me and rendering me the most miserable wretch in history. Remember my betrayal, but remember, too, the lesson I learned: man cannot impose his will on God; the way of Christ is higher and holier than we know—certainly out of the range of our impositions.

(Jesus makes spontaneous remarks to Judas.)

Reader: After Judas had left, Jesus said: "Now the Son of Man's glory is revealed; now God's glory is revealed through him. And if God's glory is revealed through him, then God himself will reveal the glory of the Son of Man, and he will do so at once. My children, I shall not be with you very much longer. You will look for me; but I tell you now what I told the Jews, 'You cannot go where I am going.' A new commandment I give you: love one another. As I have loved you, so you must love one another. If you have love for one another, then all will know that you are my disciples."

(John 13:31–35)

Matthew: Can you imagine what life is like for people who are hated because of their jobs? Allow me, Matthew, your typical tax collector, to tell you. Because my job was to levy taxes according to an individual's ability to pay, I was called greedy and unfair —among other things. I was despised to the extent that people sometimes would not let me in to worship. Yet Jesus loved me and wanted me to follow him—he sure didn't have to ask me twice! He not only replaced my original name of Levi with my new name Matthew or "gift of God," but he changed me from my old, despised self into a blessing.

(Jesus makes spontaneous remarks to Matthew.)

Reader: "Where are you going, Lord?" Simon Peter asked him. "You cannot follow me now where I am going," answered Jesus; "but later you will follow me." "Lord, why can't I follow you now?" asked Peter. "I am ready to die for you!" Jesus answered: "Are you really ready to die for me? I tell you the truth: before the rooster crows you will say three times that you do not know me."

"Do not be worried and upset," Jesus told them. "Believe in God, and believe also in me. There are many rooms in my Father's house, and I am going to prepare a place for you. I would not tell you this if it were not so. And after I go and prepare a place for you, I will come back and take you to myself, so that you will be where I am. You know how to get to the place where I am going." Thomas said to him, "Lord, we do not know where you are going; how can we know the way to get there?" Jesus answered him: "I am the way, I am the truth, I am the life; no one goes to the Father except by me. Now that you have known me," he said to them, "you will know my Father also; and from now on you do know him, and you have seen him."

(John 13:36–38, John 14:1–7)

Thomas: You probably know me as the doubter of the bunch: I'm Thomas. But do you know that I would have followed Jesus anywhere? Once I even urged the others that we band together to die with Jesus. Always hungry for truth, I often asked Jesus questions. But I was totally bewildered by his death, expressing my grief and searching for answers alone. My bewilderment was compounded, however, when I heard that Jesus had returned. My mind almost exploded with questions, doubts. But all my questions and doubts vanished when I touched our risen Lord. Bring your questions and fears to him openly and he will reveal himself to you in such a way that you will wonder what you ever had to question or to fear.

(Jesus makes spontaneous remarks to Thomas.)

Reader: Philip said to him, "Lord, show us the Father; that is all we need." Jesus answered: "For a long time I have been with you all; yet you do not know me, Philip? Whoever has seen me has seen the Father. Why, then, do you say, 'Show us the Father'? Do you not believe, Philip, that I am in the Father and the Father is in me? The words that I have spoken to you," Jesus said to his disciples, "do not come from me. The Father, who remains in me, does his own works. Believe me that I am in the Father and the Father is in me. If not, believe because of these works. I tell you the truth: whoever believes in me will do the works I do—yes, he will do even greater ones, for I am going to the Father. And I will do whatever you ask for in my name, so that the Father's glory will be shown through the Son. If you ask me for anything in my name, I will do it."

(John 14:8–24)

Philip: Do you know the first disciple that Jesus called? Me—Philip! Although I don't usually have much to say due to my shy nature, I did introduce Nathanael to Jesus and assist Andrew with his Greek delegation. But along with my quiet image, I have a surprising gift: I ask questions that need to be asked when they need to be asked. For instance, when I asked Jesus to show the Father to the Greeks, he had a chance to give them some pretty potent information—and he did! When we provide such opportunities for Christ to work, he is always ready.

(Jesus makes spontaneous remarks to Philip.)

Reader: "If you love me, you will obey my commandments. I will ask the Father, and he will give you another Helper, the Spirit of truth, to stay with you for ever. The world cannot receive him, because it cannot see him or know him. But you know him, for he remains with you and lives in you.

"I will not leave you alone; I will come back to you. In a little while the world will see me no more, but you will see me; and because I live, you also will live. When that day comes, you will know that I am in my Father, and that you are in me, just as I am in you."

(John 14:15–20)

(Pause)

Reader: When the hour came, Jesus took his place at the table with the apostles. And he said to them:

Jesus: "I have wanted so much to eat this Passover meal with you before I suffer! For I tell you, I will never eat it until it is given its real meaning in the Kingdom of God."

(Jesus picks up his cup.)

Reader: Then Jesus took the cup, gave thanks to God, and said,

Jesus: "Take this and share it among yourselves; for I tell you that I will never drink this wine from now on until the Kingdom of God comes."

(Jesus replaces his cup. He picks up loaf and breaks it.)

Reader: Then he took the bread, gave thanks to God, broke it, and gave it to them, saying,

(Jesus passes the bread.)

Jesus: "This is my body which is given for you. Do this in memory of me."

(Eat the bread.)

(Jesus picks up his cup of wine.)

Reader: In the same way he gave them the cup, after the supper, saying,

(Jesus carries his cup to one end of the table. Disciples sip and pass it on.)

Jesus: "This cup is God's new covenant sealed with my blood which is poured out for you."

(Drink the wine.)

(Luke 22:14–20)

Reader: "Whoever accepts my commandments and obeys them, he is the one who loves me. My Father will love him who loves me; I too will love him and reveal myself to him."

Judas (not Judas Iscariot) said, "Lord, how can it be that you will reveal yourself to us and not to the world?" Jesus answered him: "Whoever loves me will obey my message. My Father will love him, and my Father and I will come to him and live with him. Whoever does not love me does not obey my words. The message you have heard is not mine, but comes from the Father who sent me."

(John 14:21–24)

Thaddaeus: My name is Thaddaeus, but I am also known as Judas, the son of James. One of the most noticeable things about me is my curiosity: I ask lots of questions. When I asked Jesus why he had revealed himself only to the twelve of us and not to the whole world, I found out that people must be receptive before such a revelation can occur. How could anyone fail to be receptive to Jesus, I wondered. He is ready to give himself to all who ask him to be their Lord.

(Jesus makes spontaneous remarks to Thaddaeus.)

Reader: I have told you this while I am still with you. The helper, the Holy Spirit whom the Father will send in my name, will teach you everything, and make you remember all that I have told you.

(John 14:25–26)

Bartholomew: I too have two names: Bartholomew and Nathanael. When Jesus first met me, he said, "Here is an Israelite; there is nothing false in him." I knew him as the Son of God almost immediately and proclaimed him to be the king of Israel on the spot. As I followed Christ, I came to understand that he knows the real you and the real me, including our loyalty levels and sincerity quotients. We can't hide anything from him, and yet he loves us—always!

(Jesus makes spontaneous remarks to Bartholomew.)

Jesus: "Peace I leave with you; my own peace I give you. I do not give it to you as the world does. Do not be worried and upset;

do not be afraid. You heard me say to you, 'I am leaving, but I will come back to you.' If you loved me, you would be glad that I am going to the Father, because he is greater than I. I have told you this now, before it all happens, so that when it does happen you will believe. I cannot talk with you much longer, for the ruler of this world is coming. He has no power over me, but the world must know that I love the Father; that is why I do everything as he commands me. Rise, let us go from this place."

(John 14:27–31)
(The first-person portraits are paraphrased from
The Good Friday Service of Tenebrae, by Ferrel)

Reflections

Knowing the needs of your worship community is very important. We felt that our people were not yet prepared to experience foot washing, so we substituted hands for feet and found a gentle, loving experience—nonthreatening, but valid.

When Jesus began to speak from the Luke Scriptures, we were moved into the Communion experience. Worshipers used left-over matzo and wine for the elements. Should all these elements be gone, the disciples might refill the plates and cups for Communion.

Probably one of our simplest services in content, this you-were-there Communion is also one of the most meaningful celebrations we've experienced.

3

Jesus: The Bread of Life
(Communion)

IDEA GERM	Jesus is life's essential, symbolized by bread.
DESCRIPTION OF SERVICE	A Communion service that features the symbolism of the bread. The elements are explained and experienced thoroughly, the children having baked the bread in advance. A moving family experience.
PREPARATION CHECKLIST	Set a time and date for the children to bake bread in advance of the service. You also need a place and a person to supervise this undertaking.

Ask all children between the ages of six and fourteen to help bake bread. Use word of mouth, bulletin announcements, and postcards to spread the word. Provide transportation for those who need it.

Compile a list and purchase the needed ingredients. *Note:* Only one recipe would be needed for Communion, but we quadrupled our recipe because of the number of children involved and because we wanted each child's family to take home a loaf or a half-loaf to share.

We used the following recipe:

Whole Wheat Bread Recipe

1 pkg. yeast in ¼ cup warm water	3 tbsp. shortening
½ cup brown sugar	1 tbsp. salt
	1 cup boiling water

Stir in a large bowl until dissolved, except for yeast.

Add:

1 cup cold water   Softened yeast

Sift gradually.

Add:

4 cups whole wheat flour   1½ to 2 cups plain flour

Knead 5 or 6 minutes. Place in greased bowl and grease top. Let rise 2½ hours. Then mash down. Shape into loaves and put into greased pans. Bake 45 minutes at 325–350 degrees.

Note: Our pastor's wife supervised our baking in her own kitchen, an added benefit for our children, who seldom know her in this setting. We set up two shifts of children: one to mix and one to punch and shape. The pastor's wife and worship coordinator completed the baking and wrapping, but the children warmed the bread in the church oven just before the actual Communion.

Ask your minister to speak informally to the children on baking day. Their understanding of the significance of bread, scripturally and symbolically, is important. Also, clear the minister's role in conducting the Communion service with him.

Recruit a leader, an adult reader, and a family for "the lighting of the Advent wreath."

Provide Advent wreath, matches, etc.

Notify musicians of song selections.

Ask a dancer to interpret "The Baker Woman." See that she gets the record well in advance for rehearsal.

Make room arrangements using the Communion elements as your focus. *Note*: We used a circular arrangement so that everyone could see our dancer. The Communion table was placed at one side of the circle.

Be sure the record player is handy and ready to go.

Design and reproduce programs including the celebration of the Communion, the service of Communion, prayer, and benediction hymn.

Add other visual aids if you wish.

Service Script: Jesus: The Bread of Life

OPENING

Leader: We're hungry for something, Lord.

We have so much rich food
and cake and candy for ourselves,
but we're hungry.

Kids around the world are starving
and we don't know how to reach them.
We're hungry for them.
We want to eat with them
and listen with them.

People around us are so stiff
and tight and hard to reach.
And they make us that way.
But we're hungry for something more.

Big people tell us
to do things their way,
always their way.
They say one thing
and do something else.
We're hungry for other things.
We want to be honest
and natural
and free.

Church people tell us
to dress a certain way,
act a certain way,
and look a certain way.
But we're hungry for fun.
We want to be alive in church
and be ourselves with God.

Preachers give us God talk,
old answers and church talk.
But we're hungry for answers
that reach inside of us,
even if they hurt us.

People around us seem strong,
and sure of themselves.
But we're hungry for people
who admit what they are,
who take off their masks
and face us as real people.

People we know
keep talking about great ideas,
brilliant questions,
and the problem of God's existence.
But we're hungry for you,
not ideas or theories.
We want you to touch us,
to reach inside us
and turn us on.

There are so many people
who will counsel us to death.
But we're hungry for someone
who really knows you
and has you,
someone who can get so close to us
that we can see you there.

We have so many things,
but we're hungry for you.
Deep, deep down inside
we're hungry,
even if we appear to be silly,
lazy, or unconcerned at times.

We're hungry for your kind of power
and love and joy.

Feed us, Lord,
feed us with your rich food.

("We're Hungry, Lord," Interrobang, Habel, pp. 24–25)

SCRIPTURE	John 6:25–35 (TEV)
CONTEM-PORARY READING	*(Excerpts from* The Gospel of John, *vol. 1, edited by William Barclay, or from another similar source)*
LIGHTING OF THE ADVENT WREATH	*(Use currently available Advent wreath services of your denomination or write your own.)*

Offering, Prayers, Community Concerns

CHILDREN SHARING EXPERIENCE OF MAKING BREAD	Children remain where they are in the worship community. *(If this service takes place with a large group in a big room, you may want the children to move closer to the leader.)*

The leader briefly tells the congregation what the children did and then lets the children respond or asks them questions.

"THE BAKER WOMAN"	An interpretive dance to recording of "The Baker Woman" on the *Go Tell Everyone* record.
CELEBRATION OF COMMUNION	

Minister: Now let us reenact the meal of our Lord, the sign and the symbol by which we are bound together as Christians: What have we brought?

All: We have brought bread.

Minister: Why bread?

Men: Bread is the food of the people of God. We remember the story of the Hebrew people when God gave them bread to eat.

Women: We remember the prophet Elijah in the desert who was given bread by an angel and restored to his strength.

Men: We remember the prophets who worked for the day when all people would have enough to eat.

Women: We remember that Jesus made 5,000 people sit down and there on the hillside he fed them with bread.

Minister: There is a mystery in bread. The grain has died in the earth and has borne fruit after its death. The death yielded hundreds of new grains. Jesus used the image for himself.

All: Yet there is a commonness in bread. Bread is the stuff of everyday life, eaten by men of many nations: eaten by the most powerful and the lowliest of peasants.

Minister: What else have we brought?

All: We have the fruit of the vine.

Men: Wine is the drink of the people of God. Created to delight us, it represents the death of a thousand grapes.

Women: Wine reminds us of suffering. The grapes are trodden underfoot and ruthlessly destroyed, like so many people are.

Men: When we drink it, flashes of memory and association remind us of the history of God and his people.

Women: We remember Joshua coming back from Canaan with the giant grapes of the promised land.

Men: The story of Jesus at the wedding where he made more wine than the party could drink.

Women: And the joy which surrounded the early Christians in their weekly celebrations of Christ's resurrection.

Minister: We are reminded also that many have given of themselves that we may have bread and wine.

All: We are reminded that every day of our lives we are dependent on the giving of others.

> (A litany from United University Church, Minneapolis, Minn.)

HYMN   "Take Our Bread"

> (Songbook for Saints and Sinners, Young, p. 25)

Minister: The Lord Jesus, on the night he was betrayed, took the bread, gave thanks to God, broke it, and said, "This is my body which is given for you. Do this in memory of me." In the same way, he took the cup after the supper and said, "This cup is God's new covenant, sealed with my blood. Whenever you drink it, do it in memory of me." For until the Lord comes, you proclaim his death whenever you eat this bread and drink from this cup.

(I Cor. 11:23f, TEV)

All: We lift up these common elements of life, O Lord, as symbols of all you have created. We lift them up as representative of the incarnation of your Word in Jesus Christ. We lift them up as the communicators of those deeps which are the ultimate mystery of our lives. Consecrate them to the task for which they are intended. Amen.

Minister: Now eat, all who would be restored to wholeness of life.

All: Let us serve our fellow man, saying: "This body of Christ is broken for you."

(Here the bread is passed and he who passes shall repeat these words to his neighbor.)

(After all have shared in the bread and wine:)

Minister: Are you satisfied?

All: We are humbled and healed. We have received the brokenness and poured-out-ness of our Lord and his creation. We have received new life. We are satisfied and give thanks.

PRAYER

All: God,
We pray, in the prayer taught to us by Jesus, for our daily bread. We recognize the need we have for bread. We recognize

that people the world over are hungry. Our population is ever increasing. We seek ways to make known that your son Jesus provides us with the essential, with the bread of life. As we prepare to share the bread of life in the hungry world we ask that even now we receive a portion for our own daily living. Fill us, O God, this day!

BENEDICTION

People: Feed us, Lord.

Minister: Feed us with your rich food.

("We're Hungry, Lord," Interrobang, *Habel, p. 25*)

All: Amen

Reflections

Baking the bread will take a whole day. Our older children were our punchers and shapers and were not too challenged, so our preacher's wife came up with the idea of taking the bread out of the oven about ten minutes early. Then we let the older group warm the bread in the church oven right before the service.

We did see, however, just how meaningful the baking experience had been for them when they proudly picked up their loaves and presented them to their families after the service.

The comments of William Barclay on this Scripture (John 6:25-35) are particularly good. Thus we included excerpts from these as contemporary readings.

A record was used for the dancing of "The Baker Woman." An effective alternate benediction would be to sing together the refrain from "The Baker Woman."

If possible, some form of indirect lighting would lend itself well to the atmosphere.

During the children's sharing experience, the leader should be prepared to ask specific questions of the children concerning their experience. Be aware that the responses may not be those you expect; e.g., one child said, "It was gooey!"

4

And It Came to Pass
(Advent)

IDEA GERM	To visualize the prophecy of Isaiah being fulfilled by Jesus' life.
DESCRIPTION OF SERVICE	An artist draws his interpretation of Jesus' hands during the various stages of life while the congregation reads about those same stages and listens to appropriate music selections.
PREPARATION CHECKLIST	Find an artist and discuss this project with him, allowing him some time for creative reaction. Our man provided his own materials.

Prepare a musical background tape, coordinating the length with time the artist needs for each hand or set of hands.

Be sure tape and equipment are in place and ready to go before service starts.

Contact a family to do the Advent wreath candlelighting service.

Recruit a leader to begin Scripture readings. (It may be the same person who reads Eph. 2:19 and prays.)

Notify musicians of song selections.

Provide Advent wreath and matches to be set on worship center. Place to one side so as not to interfere with the artist's work.

See that the bulletin cover is designed and the bulletins prepared.

Arrange seating for the best possible view. Tiered seating is a possibility, as is raising the artist on a platform.

Service Script: And It Came to Pass

CALL TO
WORSHIP

"Hey! Hey! Anybody Listening?"

> (Hymns Hot and Carols Cool, *Avery and Marsh, p. 5*)

LIGHTING OF
THE ADVENT
WREATH

(Use currently available Advent wreath service of your denomination, or write your own.)

SCRIPTURE

Eph. 2:19 (RSV)

(Start tape here: "And the Glory of the Lord," "Behold a Virgin Shall Conceive," "O, Thou that Tellest")

PRAYER

THE PROPHECY
AND THE
FULFILLMENT

Isa. 11:1–2
(Read collectively just before end of "O, Thou that Tellest.")

All: There shall come forth a shoot from the stump of Jesse, and a branch shall grow out of his roots. And the Spirit of the Lord shall rest upon him . . .

THE INFANT

Isa. 9:6

(As "For Unto Us a Child Is Born" begins on tape, artist begins sketch of baby hands, and congregation reads:)

All: For to us a child is born, to us a son is given; and the government will be upon his shoulder, and his name will be called "Wonderful Counselor, Mighty God, Everlasting Father, Prince of Peace."

THE CHILD

Luke 2:41–43, 52

(As "Pastoral Symphony" plays on tape, artist draws boy's hands and the congregation reads:)

All: Now his parents went to Jerusalem every year at the feast of the Passover. And when he was twelve years old, they went up according to custom; and when the feast was ended, as they were returning, the boy Jesus stayed behind in Jerusalem . . . And Jesus increased in wisdom and in stature, and in favor with God and Man.

THE
CARPENTER   Mark 6:2–3
(Artist sketches carpenter's hands during "He Shall Feed His Flock" and the congregation reads:)

All: And on the sabbath he began to teach in the synagogue; and many who heard him were astonished, saying, "Where did this man get all this? What is the wisdom given to him? What mighty works are wrought by his hands! Is not this the carpenter, the son of Mary . . ."

THE TEACHER   Mark 1:21–22

("His Yoke Is Easy" plays on tape while artist draws the teacher's hands and the congregation reads:)

All: And they went into Capernaum; and immediately on the sabbath he entered the synagogue and taught. And they were astonished at his teaching, for he taught as one who had authority. . . .

THE SAVIOR   Isa. 53:1–3

(Tape plays "Behold, the Lamb of God" while artist draws Savior's hands and the congregation reads:)

All: Who has believed what we have heard? And to whom has the arm of the Lord been revealed? For he grew up before him like a young plant, and like a root out of dry ground; he had no form or comeliness that we should look at him, and no beauty that we should desire him. He was despised and rejected by men; a man of sorrows, and acquainted with grief; and as one from whom men hide their faces he was despised, and we esteemed him not.

THE BENEDICTION

Rev. 5:12

(Tape plays "I Know That My Redeemer Liveth" and "Worthy Is the Lamb" during and after the benediction:)

All: "Worthy is the Lamb who was slain, to receive power and wealth and wisdom and might and honor and glory and blessing! (Amen!)

Reflections

The person who leads the collective readings must be strong in indicating when to begin. This person must be very familiar with the tape you use and must be firm in getting the people's attention so that their thoughts can focus on the Scripture and then return to the artist.

Our artist allowed ten minutes for each drawing but didn't really need that much time.

The drawings were signed and sprayed and have since been matted for display in the church.

The tape we used was arranged as follows:

> "And the Glory of the Lord,"
> "Behold a Virgin Shall Conceive,"
> "O, Thou that Tellest,"
> "For Unto Us a Child Is Born,"
> "The Pastoral Symphony,"
> "He Shall Feed His Flock,"
> "His Yoke Is Easy,"
> "Behold, the Lamb of God,"
> "I Know That My Redeemer Liveth," and
> "Worthy Is the Lamb."

There were no pauses on this tape between selections.

5

Whither Shall I Go from Thy Presence?
(Advent)

IDEA GERM	Advent is a season which often is difficult to celebrate worshipfully. This service is meant to reassure people that God is in all aspects of this season, "religious" or not.
DESCRIPTION OF SERVICE	Special music, visual aids, and candlelighting add a bit of chaos to this service, providing just the right atmosphere for the reading about worship distractions and the multimedia meditation about distractions of the Advent season. Everyone should be able to identify with this colorful and interesting service.
PREPARATION CHECKLIST	Recruit ten readers as "voices." (Can be done with six if necessary.) *Rehearsal is a must.*

Arrange for pastor to do the meditation. Be sure to set a time for him to see the slides and hear the sounds so that he will be fully aware of all that's going to happen.

Notify musicians of song selection in time for them to rehearse.

Ask director of music to prepare anthem with either full choir or choir ensemble.

Arrange to have slides taken and sounds recorded for meditation. Be sure the sights and sounds depicted coordinate somewhat. Use sound-effect records or tape your own sound effects, e.g., a baby's laugh and cry, Salvation Army band music, sirens, crowds, etc.

Arrange your worship room. Be sure to have slides and tape and tape player ready to go.

Use visual aids.

Service Script: Whither Shall I Go from Thy Presence?

OPENING
HYMN

"The King of Glory"

(New Wine: Songs for Celebration, Strathdee and Stringer, p. 13)

STATEMENT OF
EMPHASIS

"In the beginning, God created the heavens and the earth . . . and God saw that it was good."

Both Judaism and Christianity have their basis in the book that begins with the assertion that all things come from one source; and in their theologies and philosophies they sometimes elaborate that all of creation partakes of the goodness of God's own existence—and is indeed good, as the writer of Genesis has God himself testifying.

And yet—in a civilization that is dominated by these religions—men paradoxically have led schizophrenic lives separating "religion" and "the world."

Religious men were not supposed to have much concern for this life and for this world; and religious men who wanted to be totally dedicated to God did so by entering monasteries, withdrawing from society where concern for other men detracted from their concern for God.

Furthermore, we find in Scripture that there is *no way of serving or loving God directly. We must serve him by serving our fellow man.*

We must take down once and for all that artificial barrier, that iron curtain which separates the sacred and the secular, that keeps God from his world. We must learn more thoroughly and more concretely the implications of the Incarnation —that we do not have to be less manly to become more Godly, no more than Christ had to be less Godly to be more manly. The concept of a God-out-there-somewhere must not get in the way of our discovering the God who is the root and ground of all being.

In our actions, religion and life, spirit and matter, intellect and emotion, heaven and earth, the sacred and the secular, the natural and the supernatural are reconciled once more. Our efforts are real acts of *atonement*, at-one-ment. Our efforts are indeed sacramental, not only symbolizing but effecting salvation! It is these efforts that we celebrate.

For centuries we have been singing at the dedication of a Church: "How awe-inspiring is this place! This is none other than the house of God! This is the very gate of heaven!" Today we sing these words in the rededication of total, integral human society with all its art and technology. For this world is the very house of God. This is our gate to heaven. "How awe-inspiring is this place!"

(from Celebration, Rivers, *pp. 10, 14, 34)*

OLD
TESTAMENT
READING   (Ps. 139:7-12, RSV)

VOICES   *(A Service of Christian Worship—If possible use a narrator, a worshiper, and eight voices. But six persons may present the service by using only four voices—each voice taking two parts. Number 1 could read parts 1 and 5, number 2 could read parts 2 and 6, and so forth.*

The narrator may stand at the lectern. The worshiper may be seated in the front (center) pew. The voices may be seated facing each other in the chancel, the voice number 1 standing, facing an open door or window.

There should be variation in the successive voices. If number 1 is low, number 2 may be high. The worshiper should speak slowly and deliberately, attempting in spite of what he hears and sometimes because of what he hears, to worship God. It would be well to practice this service several times in order for it to be well presented.)

Narrator: And it came to pass that a man went up from his factory, his fields, his firm, his teaching to give expression to his faith in the house of God.

While he was at worship the world he supposed he had left outside and at home was not out-of-mind. Even in his moments of attempted meditation the world dinned its wares and wiles in his ears.

Voices kept calling from every source that touches the five senses of men. And his worship was interrupted and halted.

It isn't easy to worship in our world, But it never was easy to worship . . .

Worshiper: The Lord is in his holy temple, Let all the earth keep silence before him.

1. People shout
2. Cars run and horns blow
3. A dog barks
4. Motors roar
5. Jets crack the sound barrier
6. Sounds of men against men
   And men against the elements
   Shatter the stillness of the day
   And clatter on through the night.

Narrator: The earth is no temple, And its stillness is gone. A man wants to worship but he can't get far enough away from the working world.

Worshiper: O worship the Lord in the beauty of holiness . . .

Narrator: But the beauty is betrayed and the stillness is startled

1. Get a move on out there—You haven't got all day
2. Why don't you guys clam it
3. They've inaugurated a new President
4. And a Vice President,
5. And governors,
6. And senators,
7. And judges,
8. And tax collectors.

1. Will we have prosperity?
2. Will he lower taxes?
3. What will we get for our state?
4. For our town?

     5. For ourselves?
     6. For me?

Narrator: America will move forward . . .

     7. Nobody thinks he moves anywhere but forward—Except the lowly crab
     1–2–3. And he doesn't think . . .
     4–5–6. He moves—backward
     7. But he moves by design—
     8. Predestined I'd say.

Narrator: There's no predestination about the movements of man.

     1. They're not moving anywhere out there.
     2. They're not moving anything.
     3. Our tax moneys are going down the drain.

Worshiper: O Lord open thou my lips and my mouth shall show forth thy praise.

Narrator: Lips are not stilled
Mouths are open.
Ears are tuned to the wave length of the world
Listen! You can hear their voices now . . .

     1. Buy now and pay later!
     2. It's later than you think!
     3. Every thinking man needs a filter!

Narrator: And by the time a man's thinker is filtered
He needs to filter out the froth and foam of frantic frills;
To filter fact from fantasy, filter truth from untruth.
It takes a special kind of equipment to get at the truth.
It takes more than a truth squad to get at the truth.

Worshiper: Jesus said to those who believed on him, "If you continue in my word, you are truly my disciples, and you will know the truth and the truth will make you free." "I am the way and the truth and the life."

     1. It's pretested
     2. It has the good house-leaping seal of approval
     3. Consumer's Research says:
     4. Television—Vista vision—Extra vision—3-D
     5. Bifocals—Trifocals—Contact lenses

Worshiper: And Jesus answered them, "Go and tell John what you hear and see: the blind receive their sight and the lame walk, lepers are cleansed and the deaf hear, and the dead are raised up, and the poor have good news preached to them."

Narrator: Women appreciate dash!

6. Dash does almost anything—It's the cleanest wash in town.

Narrator: So the dash to cleanliness is on
Led by a man with an accent
To whom wash and dash
Are far more foreign than cash.

7. Cash payments? No! They give you time
8. All the time you want!
2. Pay the rest of your life.
1. It's a sentence!

Narrator: We are asked to keep clean and save cash
Hardly anyone asks us to *come clean* and *give cash*.

Worshiper: Create in me a clean heart, O God, and put a new and right spirit within me. Cast me not away from thy presence and take not thy holy Spirit from me.

Narrator: We're asked at every turn of the knob, or the aisle—
Keep clean with cleenies
And save cash
With a dash to go out and buy.

1. A $14.98 value for only $11.98
2. Special today, try the put-it-off way
3. Five loaves for a dollar
4. Buy now and save
5. Call in today and come in tomorrow
6. Buy one box and get a second free
7. Buy $5 worth of groceries and get fifty free stamps

All: Top value stamps—Gold Bond stamps—Redemption stamps—Brown stamps—Eagle stamps—Yellow stamps—Green stamps—Pink stamps—TV stamps

1. TV time, any good time is distaff time

Narrator: So time gets tied to the free and easy, and the irresponsible!
And values are subjected to what gives pleasure.
All of this happens as one plays, and eats, and rides.
Everywhere there is the postponement of the pain of paying.

Worshiper: He that would save his life shall lose it and he that would lose
his life for my sake and the gospel's shall save it.

Narrator: The voices and the vices of men are companions in crime.
Insane isn't it
And then people tell us they don't like to be preached to,
They don't like to be counseled with,
They don't like being told.

1. Write a thirty-page term paper
2. I'll write my girl instead
3. Read six chapters of history
4. I'll go out and make some history of my own
5. Get to work on time all the time
6. I'd rather go to (Howard Johnson's)
7. Develop habits of personal prayer life
8. I've got the habits, but they don't run in that line.
4. Help stamp out thirst
1. Drink
2. Drink Coca-Cola, Pepsi-Cola, beer.
3. Drink coffee, cocoa, tea.

Narrator: Occasionally they ask one to drink milk—But nobody's pushing
water.

Worshiper: O God thou art my God, I seek thee,
My soul thirsts for thee;
My flesh faints for thee
As a dry and weary land, where no water is
Blessed are they who do hunger and thirst after righteousness

5. Tensions mount up
4. Nerves on edge

Worshiper: "Be not anxious for the morrow, for the morrow will be anxious
for itself."

6. Take two spoonfuls, stir, serve hot, drink one cup.

Worshiper: But Jesus said to the disciples, "You do not know what you are asking. Are you able to drink the cup that I drink . . . ?"

7. Get your paper here—

All: Read all about it!

8. Extra! Extra!

All: Read all about it!

1. Special K gives you vitamins for the day.

Narrator: But there's another special K in our day—It's Kosygin they say—a Communist
Seemingly covering the earth with more meaningful sounds
More realistic sounds—More understandable sounds

Narrator: The worshiper cries out

Worshiper: God be merciful to me a sinner

Narrator: But the voices drone on:

2. What do doctors do?
3. What do doctors say?
4. Three out of four recommend!
5. Are you fatigued!
6. They recommend themselves!
7. Is your blood tired?
8. They recommend their products!
1. Are you a concerned person?

Narrator: They recommend sickness you haven't got!
For pills you ought to get—

Half of Group: Take Anacin, aspirin, apples, Arrid, anything.

Other Group: Take Bismol, Bufferin, Bisodol

Narrator: Someone's got to sell
To sooth the nerves
Relax tension

Add a hint of mint and do your little stint for our company.
Men must buy and sell and eat and drink
They must convey and converse
They must have companies
But they also need another kind of company.

Worshiper: Truly ye are my disciples if ye do the will of him that sent me. Come unto me all ye that labor—take my yoke upon you and follow me.

Narrator: Men need silence too . . . a time to reflect, to repent, to return. . . . The world presents its sights and sounds constantly day and night. They are dinned in our ears. Man cannot completely remove himself from his world. But he can bring the cares and concerns of the world of men before the judgment and mercy of God.

Worshiper: God be merciful to me a sinner. Take not thy holy Spirit from me.

Narrator: Jesus knew the cares and troubles of the world.
The crowds pressed in upon him from every side
"And when they could not get near him because of the crowd, they removed the roof above him and let down the pallet on which the paralytic lay."
"How can we feed these men," his disciples asked . . . *(Pause)*
He asked, *(pause)* "How many loaves have you?"

All: It isn't easy to worship in our world—But it never was. One tries to get away from the world—But the world is the concern of Christians.

(Voices, by Rumpf)

ANTHEM   "He Comes to Us as One Unknown"

(words by Schweitzer, music by Marshall)

LIGHTING OF   *Note: Use currently available Advent wreath services of your*
THE ADVENT   *denomination, or write your own.*
WREATH

Offering and Concerns

NEW
TESTAMENT
READING

I Tim. 4:4–5 (TEV)

MEDITATION

Pastor's message—ten minutes—depicting community activities. Slides of all types of ordinary community activities during the Advent season and tape of sounds presented while he speaks.

DISMISSAL
HYMN

"Go Tell It on the Mountain"

(The Methodist Hymnal, *p. 404*)

Reflections

Voices must be rehearsed several times in advance. Our host family was in charge of this part of the service. They invited a few friends to help them, and the reading was very effective.

The meditation is a gentle use of multimedia, right for our worship community. It is an adaptation of an idea from *New Forms of Worship* by James White.

A variety of sound-effect records and tapes (8-track and cassette) are available.

6

And They Came to See
(Christmas)

IDEA GERM

To celebrate the wonder and joy of the Christmas event and to point up its never-ending relevancy in our lives.

DESCRIPTION
OF SERVICE

This service has the look of a traditional Christmas worship hour until the minister is half through the reading of the Christmas story. At that point a rather startling invasion is launched—by the shepherds and one of the wise men of old. They perform a playlet that sets the scene for the minister's sermon. After such glad sharing about the baby Jesus' arrival, the people eagerly pray and sing their service to an end.

PREPARATION
CHECKLIST

Ask your minister to deliver a ten-minute sermon on whatever he most wants to say about Christmas. Explain about the interruption and playlet and his role in the prayer that follows.

Recruit actors for the playlet: the old man (who can sing), the boy, the first shepherd, the second shepherd, and the wise man.

Mimeograph the playlet and see that each character has a copy and rehearses.

Provide simple costumes—bathrobe and sandal variety, with something slightly more elegant for the wise man. Staves are appropriate for the shepherds and the old man.

Ask a family to light the Advent candle. Perhaps this family would be responsible for getting the props and setting up the worship center.

Tell the musicians which song selections to practice and also make arrangements for the special music. A duet with guitar accompaniment is effective.

See that the bulletins, cover and content, are prepared.

Set up special seating for the playlet characters. Their seats should be placed up front but off to the side, so they can be seen and heard during the dramatization but also can become part of the listening community afterwards.

Service Script: And They Came to See

CALL TO
WORSHIP

"Hey! Hey! Anybody Listening?"

(Hymns Hot and Carols Cool, Avery and Marsh, p. 5)

LIGHTING OF
THE ADVENT
WREATH

(Use currently available Advent wreath service of your own denomination, or write your own.)

Offering and Community Concerns

SPECIAL MUSIC

"The Virgin Mary Had a Baby Boy"

(Songbook for Saints and Sinners, Young, p. 44)

SCRIPTURE

Luke 2:1–7 (read by minister from RSV)

(At approximate middle of the Scripture, faint music [introduction to "The Oxen"] is heard. Supported by the boy and a staff, the old man enters slowly while singing "The Oxen." ["The Oxen" is found in Vaughn Williams's Hodie.] The other characters follow. The minister registers shock at seeing these people and being interrupted in his reading.)

AND THEY
CAME TO SEE

First
Shepherd: It's good to see you, old one.

Old Man: And you, too. (Pause)

Boy: Why do we meet like this every year, in different places, to hear what other people say? I remember what happened in Bethle-hem. I remember everything.

First Shepherd: My son, we were the first who came to see that child called Jesus. We were called to see a miracle. And because we were the first, we return to—as you say—hear what those who were not there say. We are looking for something other than a re-counting of an old and familiar story.

Second Shepherd: Yes, we hear about the baby Jesus, and how he was born in a stable and how some unknown shepherds were the first to recognize him. We hear ourselves spoken of as characters in a beautiful story, but somehow we hope to hear about the reality of our existence.

Boy: But we were real! We were there!

Old Man: My son, time and distance work their changes in all of us, even in me and I was there with you so long ago. How much more do these things affect people who only hear the story handed down over many generations. I come to recall, but these people come to discover, for the first time, the joy I know.

Boy: (*Turning to the Wise Man*)

Why did you come then? Why did you come so far? And why do you come back every year?

Wise Man: That first time, I traveled many miles, looking for a king who would, perhaps, right the wrongs in this world. I did not expect what I found: the promise of true righteousness and liberation for men and women, regardless of their social condition. Why do I come back every year? I suppose (*pause*) to see if the promise I first saw is being fulfilled.

Old Man: Christmas Eve and twelve of the clock . . .

"Now they are all on their knees,"
An elder said as we sat in a flock
By embers in heart side ease.

We pictured the meek mild creatures where
They dwelt in their strawy pen,
Nor did it occur to one of us there
To doubt they were kneeling then.

So fair a fancy few would weave
In these years! Yet, I feel
If someone said on Christmas Eve,
"Come; see the oxen kneel,

In the lonely barton by yonder coomb
Our childhood used to know,"
I should go with him in the gloom,
Hoping it might be so.

(from The Oxen, Thomas Hardy)

First
Shepherd: Old man, it's time. They are waiting.

Old Man: (Turns to preacher)
Tell me again. Tell me how it was.

(And They Came to See, Walker and Walker)

AND THEY   (A sermon)
CAME TO SEE (The minister responds to the playlet and proceeds with his sermon as the players listen.)

SINGING   "Go Tell It on the Mountain"

(The Methodist Hymnal)

"Little Baby Boy"

(Hymns Hot and Carols Cool, Avery and Marsh, pp. 7–8)

"Mary, Mary"

(Hymns Hot and Carols Cool, p. 9)

PRAYER   God cares about the world. I pray . . .

(Led by the minister and shared by all who wish to respond.)

BENEDICTION "I Am the Light of the World"
SONG
(The Genesis Songbook, Young, p. 32)

7

Let Me Tell You about This Family
(Christmas Communion)

IDEA GERM
To relate to the holy family as real people: the baby laughing and crying, the parents proud, protective, attending to the baby's needs.

DESCRIPTION
OF SERVICE
A strangely moving Communion service based on a simple technique. A family—mother, father, and baby—pose as the holy family. They arrive late and sit in front of and facing the congregation, but they wear their own clothes and act just as they would if seated with the rest (listen, take care of the baby, etc.). The minister talks about the holy family as people, and suddenly their humanness comes alive. The Communion that follows will long be remembered.

PREPARATION
CHECKLIST
Find a family to light the Advent candles. Let them gather the needed props.

Find another family to be the holy family for the hour—mother, father, and baby.

Ask the minister to prepare a ten-minute sermon discussing the reality of the holy family and to lead the Communion service.

Decide whether the minister or a lay person will read the Scriptures, and line up that person.

Inform the musicians of the song selections. They may prepare the special music or contact a soloist. Since this service makes different uses of music, be sure the musicians are told about these uses.

See that a colorful bulletin is produced.

Give attention to the worship center as it will be in three parts:

Advent wreath and candles, seats for the "holy family" and the minister, and the Communion elements. The family should be visible to everyone. Perhaps the Communion elements could be placed on a low table in front of them.

Use whatever visual aids seem appropriate.

Service Script: Let Me Tell You About This Family

CALL TO WORSHIP	"Hey, Hey, Anybody Listening?"
	(Hymns Hot and Carols Cool, Avery and Marsh, p. 5)

LIGHTING OF THE ADVENT WREATH	(Use currently available Advent wreath service of your denomination, or write your own.)

Offering and Community Concerns

("Holy Family" arrives during offering. They wear street clothes and attend to their baby's needs.)

SCRIPTURE	Matt. 1:18–25 (The Living Bible)
SONG	"What Child Is This?"
	(The Methodist Hymnal, p. 385)

LET ME TELL YOU ABOUT THIS FAMILY	Ten-minute sermon by the minister reflecting on the holy family as people.
SPECIAL MUSIC	"This Little Babe"
	(Alive and Singing, Avery and Marsh, p. 6)

All: Almighty God, the Father of our Lord Jesus Christ, how dare we enter into communion with the Spirit of the Christ Child without seeking his redeeming light and salvation?

How dare we offer ourselves as living sacrifices before him without any acceptance of commitment and self-giving?

How dare we approach his presence without yielding to the power of his grace and truth?

Lord, we are too unworthy of the gift of the Christ Child. He is so innocent—we are so selfish, corruptible. Yet, he was given for sinners such as ourselves for redemption . . . love . . . hope.

Lord, challenge our faith to mature beyond the simplicity of the manger child to the acceptance of the crucified man. For only then will we comprehend the true meaning of Christian discipleship and inherit the crown of eternal life. Amen.

(Prayer by James Weekley from Ventures in Worship 2, *edited by Randolph, p. 158)*

Leader: "So then, my brothers, because of God's many mercies to us, I make this appeal to you: Offer yourselves as a living sacrifice to God, dedicated to his service and pleasing to him. This is the true worship that you should offer."

(Rom. 12:1, TEV)

People: We offer this bread,
We offer this cup,
We offer ourselves,
To be united with the one full, perfect, and sufficient offering of Jesus Christ, who, the night before he offered himself for us, took bread, gave thanks to God, broke it, and said, "This is my body, which is given for you, do this in remembrance of me."

In the same way, he took the cup after the supper and said,

"Drink it, all of you, for this is my blood, which seals God's promise, my blood poured out for you and for many for the forgiveness of sins. Whenever you drink it, do it in remembrance of me."

Therefore, taking this bread and this cup in remembrance of him, we lift up our hearts and give thanks to God.

Leader: You are the Lord. All things are yours.
You give us life. You give us the world.

People sing: Go, tell it on the mountain,
Over the hills and everywhere . . .

Leader: Though we have sinned, You love us still.
You gave your Son to be a man.

People sing: Go tell it on the mountain,
Over the hills and everywhere . . .

Leader: He shared our life. He is the way.
He suffered and died for you and me.

People sing: Go tell it on the mountain,
Over the hills and everywhere . . .

Leader: He rose from the dead. He lives with you.
You sent your Spirit to live with us.

People sing: Go tell it on the mountain,
Over the hills and everywhere . . .

Leader: Blow, Holy Wind. Burn, Holy Fire.
This bread his Body. This cup his blood.

Come, Lord Jesus. Come in your power.
Come in your victory. May all be one.

Join us with all men and creation,
Past, present, and future. . . . As now we sing . . .

All sing: Go, tell it on the mountain,
Over the hills and everywhere,

Go, tell it on the mountain,
That Jesus Christ is born.

(adapted from "The Lord's Supper," Ventures in Worship 3, edited by Randolph, p. 121)

THE
INVITATION
AND THE
LORD'S SUPPER

SILENT
MEDITATION

BENEDICTION
SONG

Leader: Slaves are we and looking for a master,
Why don't you call him Lord?

People: Let's all call him Lord!

Leader: We, like our sheep need someone to guide us,
Why don't you call him Shepherd?

People: Let's all call him Shepherd!

Leader: Hungry and poor we need someone to save us,
Why don't you call him Savior?

People: Let's all call him Savior!

Leader: Kings of the world we seek someone to rule us,
Why don't you call him King?

People: Let's all call him King!

(from "Mary, Mary," Hymns Hot and Carols Cool, Avery and Marsh, p. 9)

Reflections

Our "holy family" was as natural as possible, wearing their own clothes (baby's perhaps more casual than usual for Sunday). Their conspicuous arrival during the offering drew attention to them as they found their places, took off coats, deposited diaper bag, etc. Then they were ready to comfort, feed, rock to sleep—whatever their baby needed. Our baby happened to be fascinated by a candle flame, however, and enjoyed the whole thing tremendously.

In his sermon, our minister reflected on the emotions of these people, letting us identify with Joseph's pain and finally his acceptance of Mary's pregnancy, her exhaustion on the trip to Bethlehem, his concern for her as they arrived and labor began, their feelings as new parents, etc. Attention centered on the baby through the special song, "This Little Babe."

The family further served as symbolic hosts at the Communion table.

These program events were easily understood and very moving. And the benediction, sung by the minister with a response from everyone, was particularly effective.

8

A Walk with Jesus

IDEA GERM	To experience the reality of walking with Jesus. To imagine how we would behave if Jesus strolled along with us side by side.
DESCRIPTION OF SERVICE	The congregation searches for a closeness with Jesus in today's world. With the minister posing as Jesus and explaining the Beatitudes, slides of your town flash by and new perspectives form. The familiar but not until now connected words and sights blend to localize a portion of the ever-powerful Sermon on the Mount.
PREPARATION CHECKLIST	Have a roll of slides made of scenes in your city that illustrate each Beatitude. For example, some pictures of babies could be used for the "pure in heart" section.
	Ask the pastor to be Jesus and to deliver a sermon, based on the Beatitudes, in the first person.
	Inform the guitarist or other musicians of the song selection. These people also may be responsible for the special music; or a soloist or very small ensemble would be effective.
	Arrange for either a host family or leader to be in charge of the greeting, offering, Scriptures, etc.
	Set up the room to suit your circumstances. You may want to use a half-circle with a center aisle for showing the slides. If so, place the worship center to one side, leaving space for the minister to enter opposite.

Have the bulletin designed and mimeographed or printed.

Service Script: A Walk with Jesus

PRELITURGY
SONG

"Just a Closer Walk with Thee"

(Genesis Songbook, *Young, p. 65*)

GREETINGS AND
COMMUNITY
INTERESTS AND
CONCERNS

Offering

Leader: So then, as we have opportunity, let us do good to all men, and especially to those who are of the household of faith.

(*Gal. 6:10, RSV*)

OPENING
SCRIPTURE

Mic. 6:6–8 (RSV)

SPECIAL MUSIC

"Lonesome Valley"

(Songbook for Saints and Sinners, *Young, p. 24*)

SCRIPTURE

Matt. 16:24–25 (TEV)

PRAYER OF
THE SEARCHING
COMMUNITY

All: Eternal God, you have sent your only Son to liberate us from the plight of sin and to deliver us from the finitude of death.
You clothed him in flesh and invested in him the keys to the greater Kingdom.
He lived among us.
He identified with us.
He gave us love . . . compassion . . . joy . . . peace . . . hope . . .
But due to our failure to grasp the spiritual thrust of his message of truth . . .
we have become rich in power . . . yet poor in Spirit,

we rejoice in bigotry, . . . yet fail to mourn
    in social justices,
we are deep in pride, . . . yet shallow in humility,
we inflict cruelties in relationships . . .
    yet stand deficient in mercy,
we glutton after iniquity, . . . yet starve
    after righteousness,
we refine ourselves with false appearances, . . .
    yet remain impure in heart,
we are crafty peacemakers around conference
    tables, . . .
    yet blundering peacemakers in Christian love,
we remain complacent in unrighteousness, . . .
    yet unwilling to suffer in the cause
    of spiritual justice.
Lord, forgive us of our shallow piety and our cushioned self-righteousness.
But do give us compassion . . . mercy . . . forgiveness . . .
through Jesus Christ, our Lord. Amen.

("The Beatitudes" from Ventures in Worship 2,
edited by Randolph, p. 148, #106)

JUST A CLOSER WALK   *(A first-person sermon based on the Beatitudes.)*

(Show slides of your city to illustrate the Beatitudes during part or all of the sermon.)

CLOSING SONG   "Just a Closer Walk with Thee"

(Genesis Songbook, Young, p. 65)

BENEDICTION

People: Christ himself carried our sins on his body to the cross, so that we might die to sin and live for righteousness. By his wounds you have been healed.

(1 Pet. 2:24, TEV)

Leader: It was to this that God called you; because Christ himself suffered for you and left you an example, so that you would follow in his steps. Amen.

(1 Pet. 2:21, TEV)

Reflections

Our pastor based his sermon on the Beatitudes as he took an imaginary walk through our city. He wore a robe and sandals and carried a large, rough cross on his shoulders. Your "Jesus" should be free to structure his own walk.

"Just a Closer Walk with Thee" was a new song for our community. The guitarists sang and played this song at the beginning of the worship hour to familiarize the congregation with it, since it was to be sung later in the service.

9

This Is Your Life, Thomas

IDEA GERM
To observe belief and unbelief through a look at the life of a doubter, Thomas.

DESCRIPTION
OF SERVICE
An effective use of role-play to produce a true-to-life play without a script based on the "This Is Your Life" television show format.

PREPARATION
CHECKLIST
Find four men and four women to role-play the parts in "This Is Your Life, Thomas." Give each person the Scripture or other material that will encompass his/her area of reminiscence.

Tell musicians about music selections. A soloist or choir will be needed for the special music.

Find a reader or leader for this service—perhaps the moderator could do double duty.

See that the bulletin is prepared.

Be sure the room setup includes seating at the front for "This Is Your Life." Chairs for the moderator and Thomas should be placed slightly in front and to the left of the others. If you use a table in the informal setting, it can also be used for the worship center.

Use appropriate visual aids.

Service Script: This Is Your Life, Thomas

SCRIPTURE   John 20:24–29 (TEV)

SPECIAL MUSIC   "Master Designer"

> *(from* Tell It Like It Is *by Carmichael and Kaiser)*

READING

> *Leader:* Anyone who has ever really gotten serious about this Christianity business, who has ever stepped out on a few limbs of faith, knows what a problem *doubts* can be. Doubts can saw the limb of faith right off, causing the Christian to come crashing to the ground. They can be compared with many things:
>
> Doubts are the greasy fingerprints on your camera lens.
>
> Doubts are the dirt in your wristwatch which prevents it from keeping good time.
>
> Doubts are the gravy stains on your new white tablecloth.
>
> Doubts are the mold on that piece of bread which has been left too long in your cupboard.
>
> Doubts are the bullet holes in the windshield of your getaway car.
>
> Doubts are the keys of your piano with the ivory knocked off.
>
> Doubts are the bent dimes which clog up your Coke machine.
>
> But troublesome as they may be, doubts ultimately make us stronger by challenging us to new heights. And our Lord never lets his children be challenged too far. Doubts can never win when he is on your side in the inner battle.
>
> Praise the Lord!
>
> > *("Doubts" by Kathryn Rogers Deering from* Ventures in Worship 3, *edited by Randolph, p. 88)*

Offering and Community Concerns and Interests

SINGING   "Create in Me a Clean Heart, O God"

(New Wine: Songs for Celebration,
Strathdee and Stringer, *p. 8*)

THIS IS YOUR   *(A scriptless series of role-plays bound together in a "This Is*
LIFE, THOMAS   *Your Life" format, using four men and four women. The characters remain seated in the congregation until the moderator
calls them forward. After speaking, each character takes a seat
provided at the front. Roles are based on the following:*

Moderator—*the "Ralph Edwards" who introduces Thomas
and the others and who keeps the presentation within given
time limits.*

Thomas—*responds to each character. The Scripture given to
each of the others, plus a look at one or two good commentaries, will provide the information needed.*

Thomas's mother—*a fictional character who points out
Thomas's characteristics. Her reminiscences come mainly
from what can be learned in the commentaries. For example:
"I guess it's no wonder you questioned your Lord—you questioned me constantly as a child."*

Philip—*John 14:5–14 provides the basis for his conversation
with Thomas, perhaps needing some material from the rest
of the chapter.*

Martha (sister of Lazarus)—*John 11:1–45 provides the basis
of her recollections about her brother's resurrection.*

Mary Magdalene—*John 20:1–18 will help her recall the experience she shared with Peter and John—finding the tomb
empty and seeing the Lord.*

Peter—*John 20:19–29, 21:1–9 provides his memories of Jesus'
three appearances to the disciples—once without Thomas
and two others with him.*

Mary (mother of Jesus)—*Acts 1:1–26 will help her to recall the choice of the new disciple.*

> (The Gospel of John, *vol. 2, by William Barclay and Twelve Who Were Chosen by William Barker are two recommended commentaries all characters should consult.*)

SCRIPTURE   John 14:1–7 (TEV)

SINGING   "Seek and Ye Shall Find"

> (New Wine: Songs for Celebration, *Strathdee and Stringer, p. 56*)

BENEDICTION

All: Help me to believe that I and all men
      are precious to you.
Help me to believe in you,
      when I cannot understand your ways.
Lord, I believe. Help my unbelief.

> (Creative Brooding, *Raines, p. 111*)

Reflections

"This Is Your Life, Thomas" couldn't have been more effective. We had considered using a script but really were glad we decided on the role-play approach.

10

An Hour with Paul

IDEA GERM	To absorb something of the man, Paul, through an overview of his life and through his words.
DESCRIPTION OF SERVICE	The people remember Paul as they listen to and read some of his words. When the one who portrays Paul rises to speak, some may recognize him; but all will know Paul and his message better by the time this service is completed.
PREPARATION CHECKLIST	Look for someone who is enthusiastic and able to project Paul's feelings and attitudes during his "many-colored" life to do the first-person sermon. Paul must really come alive.

Ask the choir director to prepare the anthem.

Inform the organist or pianist of the hymn selections.

Ask a person to be service leader.

See that the bulletin is produced.

Mimeograph 1 Cor. in responsive reading form, provide enough Bibles for worshipers to use, or use the hymnal as we did.

Arrange room however you wish, experimenting with ways to help the worshiping community feel closer and more "one body."

Use appropriate visual aids, such as maps of Paul's journeys and his world.

Service Script: An Hour with Paul

GREETINGS

Leader: From: Paul, chosen by God to be Jesus Christ's missionary, and from brother Sosthenes.

To: The Christians in Corinth, invited by God to be his people and made acceptable to him by Christ Jesus. And to: All Christians everywhere, whoever calls upon the name of Jesus Christ, our Lord and theirs.

May God our Father and the Lord Jesus Christ give you all of his blessings, and great peace of heart and mind.

(*1 Cor. 1:1–3*, LB)

HYMN   "Soldiers of Christ, Arise"

(The Methodist Hymnal, *p. 282. Words based on Eph. 6:11–18*)

A CONFESSION

All: For what our human nature wants is opposed to what the Spirit wants, and what the Spirit wants is opposed to what human nature wants: the two are enemies, and this means that you cannot do what you want to do. If the Spirit leads you, then you are not subject to the law.

What human nature does is quite plain. It shows itself in immoral, filthy, and indecent actions; in worship of idols and witchcraft. People become enemies, they fight, become jealous, angry, and ambitious. They separate into parties and groups; they are envious, get drunk, have orgies, and do other things like these.

(*Gal. 5:17–21*, TEV)

SILENT
MEDITATION

WORDS OF
ASSURANCE

Leader: But the Spirit produces love, joy, peace, patience, kindness, goodness, faithfulness, humility, and self-control. There is no law against such things as these. And those who belong to Christ Jesus have put to death their human nature, with all its passions and desires. The Spirit has given us life; he must also control our lives.

(Gal. 5:22–25, TEV)

ANTHEM

"If God Be for Us" (music by McCormick, words from Rom. 8:31f)

RESPONSIVE
READING

1 Cor. 13

AN
AFFIRMATION

All: For we remember before our God and Father how you put your faith into practice, how your love made you work so hard, and how your hope in our Lord Jesus Christ is firm. We know, brothers, that God loves you and has chosen you to be his own. For we brought the Good News to you, not with words only, but also with power and the Holy Spirit, and with complete conviction of its truth. You know how we lived when we were with you; it was for your own good. You imitated us and the Lord; and even though you suffered much, you received the message with the joy that comes from the Holy Spirit. So you became an example to all believers in Macedonia and Greece. For the message about the Lord went out from you not only to Macedonia and Greece, but the news of your faith in God has gone everywhere. There is nothing, then, that we need to say. All those people speak of how you received us when we visited you, and how you turned away from idols to God, to serve the true and living God and to wait for his Son to come from heaven—his Son Jesus, whom he raised from death, and who rescues us from God's wrath that is to come.

(1 Thess. 1:3–10, TEV)

NEW
TESTAMENT
LESSON

Phil. 3:10–14

PRAYER

All: I fall on my knees before the Father, from whom every family in heaven and on earth receives its true name. I ask God, from the wealth of his glory, to give you power through his Spirit to be strong in your inner selves, and that Christ will make his home in your hearts, through faith. I pray that you may have your roots and foundations in love, and that you, together with all God's people, may have the power to understand how broad and long and high and deep is Christ's love. Yes, may you come to know his love—although it can never be fully known—and so be completely filled with the perfect fulness of God.

To him who is able to do so much more than we can ever ask for, or even think of, by means of the power working in us: to God be the glory in the church and in Christ Jesus, for all time, for ever and ever! Amen.

(Eph. 3:14b–21, TEV)

HYMN   "Rejoice, the Lord is King"

> *(The Methodist Hymnal, p. 171. Words based on Phil. 4:4)*

A SERMON   "I Am Paul"
                        (A first-person sermon in which Paul really must come alive.)

HYMN   "May the Mind of Christ, My Savior"

> *(Crusader Hymns and Hymn Stories, p. 135. Words based on Phil. 2:5)*

BENEDICTION

All: And may God, the source of patience and encouragement, enable you to have the same point of view among yourselves by following the example of Christ Jesus, so that all of you together, with one voice, may praise the God and Father of our Lord Jesus Christ.

(Rom. 15:5–6, TEV)

All: Amen.

Reflections

As Paul, our pastor drew exceptionally vivid, verbal pictures which caught us up in experiences with him. He incorporated some scriptural references to illustrate his points, which duplicated Scripture used elsewhere. Since their use was arrived at independently from us, we felt a very real sense of the working of the Holy Spirit.

The thread of Paul's words throughout the traditional form of worship gave a different kind of continuity and built strong steps toward our purpose.

Our hymns were selected from our *Methodist Hymnal*. However, these traditional hymns may be found in other denominational hymnals.

11
The Church

IDEA GERM
: What is the church? What could it be? Seek answers dealing with "was," "is," "can be," "will be," plus why and wherefore.

DESCRIPTION OF SERVICE
: People who are familiar with what the church is often have good ideas about developing the church's potential. This service asks them to translate these ideas into tangible models of what they would like the church to be, listing their reasons as they go. An intriguing project that is bound to promote much thought and discussion in progress as well as when the models are shared.

PREPARATION CHECKLIST
: Ask a leader or host family to lead this service.

Give song selections to musicians.

Gather construction paper, scissors, pencils, marking pens, tape, stiff cardboard or pasteboard, and whatever else you think might be helpful in constructing the church models.

See that bulletins are done.

See that tables are set up. These need to be large enough to hold supplies and for groups of six to work around.

Service Script: The Church

PRELITURGY
: "We Are the Church"

(Songs for the Easter People, *Avery and Marsh, p. 20*)

PRAYER

All: O God, here we are. You called us and we've come. You want us to live in your love. So we have come to worship: to listen to what you have to say to us, to give thanks for what you've done for us, and to share with you the joy you've given us. Help us to make good use of this time together. And when we go out, help us to share your love with everyone. Thank you. Amen.

(Prayer, Wesley Taylor from Ventures in Worship 3, *edited by Randolph, p. 37, #31)*

SONG

"The Church Within Us"

(Songbook for Saints and Sinners, Young, p. 10)

AFFIRMATION OF FAITH

Leader: In a time which purports to be a time of reason, but harbors within it a large measure of unwillingness to reason—

People: We seek the source of reason in Christ and his church.

Leader: In a time when we are aware of our lack of wholeness—

People: We seek the missing elements in Christ and in his church.

Leader: In a time of cynicism, mistrust, and credibility gaps—

People: We seek to place our trust in Christ and through his power to become his children and his church in more than name.

Leader: In a time when churches are often considered irrelevant because of past behavior—

People: We seek to be part of a church which is aware of and responds to the present.

(Affirmation by William Law from Ventures in Worship 3, *edited by Randolph, p. 97, #121)*

SCRIPTURE 1 Cor. 3:9–17

I Would Like the Church to Be . . .

(The worshipers are divided into groups with no more than six persons in each group. The groups then are asked to consider what they would like the church to be and to build a model from their ideas. Each group is also asked to list their reasons for designing their model the way they did. No restrictions are placed on their concepts. If they see the church as a building, or people, or the world, or whatever, then that is what they try to represent in their model.)

BENEDICTION
SONG

"We Are the Church"

(Songs for the Easter People, *Avery and Marsh, p. 20*)

(The people move into a circle to link arms while singing this song.)

Reflections

The building of the church models takes a good bit of time and is enough work for two services. We believe the community should be prepared for this service ahead of time. Perhaps the week before they should be asked to consider what they would like the church to be. Or perhaps one worship session should be devoted to discussion and model planning followed by a second session on model building.

The models produced might be set up, along with their explanations, in the church for discussion. Later, perhaps the display could be moved to a retirement home for a week or so. Then, too, they could be set up and utilized by church program-planning bodies. And finally, depending on the models themselves, you might give them to a Head Start center.

Since "We Are the Church" was a new song for us, we set a learning time in the preliturgy. Also, we used some hand and arm motions with this song. You can develop these easily, for the words suggest strong movement.

12

God's People Together
(New Members)

IDEA GERM

To consider ourselves as the worshiping family of God and to welcome a new family member.

DESCRIPTION OF SERVICE

A new member takes his vows and joins the church while the congregation reaffirms itself as the family of God. These events are accomplished through a series of shared readings, songs, and dialogue groups, leading up to a unique set of contemporary vows and responses.

PREPARATION CHECKLIST

Ask your minister to counsel with prospective members, to welcome them into the fellowship, and to lead this service.

Notify musicians of music to be used so that they can rehearse.

Decide how many group leaders you need. Contact them and set up a preworship discussion time to give out the discussion questions and to clarify the purpose of the group dialogue.

See that the prospective member(s) has a list of the vows to be used—they require previous consideration.

Mimeograph the bulletin.

Cut a piece of yarn or string for each person, plus one long piece.

Arrange dialogue-group chairs close to the walls, with worship center in the middle of the large open space. Even though groups are separated, all face center.

Use visual aids. Banners made for the occasion add a festive dimension.

Service Script: The House of Worship
Symbol of God's People Together

GATHERING

(As the people enter they are tied together two by two with pieces of yarn. A long end of yarn is left loose.)

All: "We belong to Christ by belonging to each other. Because we belong to Christ, we also belong to each other. . . . He who has chosen us also chooses those who are our brothers and sisters. . . . Because we are involved with Him, we are involved with them. And the reverse is also true: through them we move closer to Him. We cannot be loyal to Him without being loyal to them. We cannot deny them without denying Him. We might wish to avoid this horizontal belonging and cling only to Him. But we cannot do so. We belong to Christ only by belonging to each other."

(from Reshaping the Christian Life, *Raines, p. 17)*

SONG

"Clap Your Hands"

(New Wine: Songs for Celebration, *Strathdee and Stringer, p. 4)*

A THOUGHT

All: "We learn Christ's love by learning to love each other. Members of a family have to struggle to learn to love one another. . . . A bridge club or a community social group may have very little friction in its common life because very little is at stake and little personal commitment is required. . . . But in the family of Christ we are all bound together unconditionally. Our very belonging is a commitment to learn to love one another as He loves us. This kind of relationship . . . calls for more than surface smiles and the exchange of clever stories and confidences. It requires the humility to accept correction and guidance from a brother in Christ, the pain of real growth. We must forgive even those who do not forgive us; we must bear and forbear even with those (especially with those) who do not respond in kind."

"It takes great courage to love and be loved like this. . . . We learn Christ's love by learning to love one another and thus release His gracious gifts in one another."

(from Reshaping the Christian Life, *Raines, pp. 19–20)*

SONG   "They'll Know We Are Christians by Our Love"

(New Wine: Songs for Celebration, Strathdee and Stringer, p. 57)

A THOUGHT

All: *"The family of Christ is a ministering community. . . . It is in the family of Christ that each person emerges in freedom to be himself and to give his own unique gift to the fellowship. It is in the family that Christ liberates the true self of a man, so that what appears to the outsider as mundane is revealed to the brother as truly of heaven."*

(from Reshaping the Christian Life, *Raines, p. 20)*

SCRIPTURE   Eph. 4:7, 11–13, 16

Offering and Community Concerns

OFFERING RESPONSE   "Praise God from Whom All Blessings Flow"

(Hymns Hot and Carols Cool, Avery and Marsh, p. 2)

DIALOGUE GROUPS   *The purpose is to get members to examine their places in the fellowship, what the fellowship means to them, the importance of the church to them—to determine the importance of the family of God to each individual. Groups should include five to eight people.*

(Discussion leaders use the following questions:)

After the past year of pilgrimage with our God and in His Church . . .

"Are our roots deeper in God's life?"

"Does the common life which we know in Christ mean more to us than a year ago?"

"Are we willing to give ourselves to the fellowship at greater cost?"

"Or is it true that Christ and his ministry mean less as more and more areas of loneliness and uncertainty and uneasiness have been satisfied?"

"Do the people who are called by Christ and redeemed by Him seem more ordinary than in the first months of wonderment?"

"Do we now question the worth of the fellowship?"

"Does it make a real difference to us whether or not it is there for another person?"

"Do we know that if we are growing Christians then we are always growing more deeply into the lives of those who compose the Body of Christ?"

(from Call to Commitment, *O'Connor, p. 38)*

MEMBERSHIP
INTO THE
FELLOWSHIP

Joiner: "I come today to join a local expression of the Church, which is the body of those on whom the call of God rests to witness to the grace and truth of God."

People: We are with you in this venture.

Joiner: "I recognize that the function of the Church is to glorify God in adoration and sacrificial service and to be God's missionary to the world, bearing witness to God's redeeming grace in Jesus Christ."

People: Our mission is also to glorify him.

Joiner: "I believe as did Peter that Jesus is the Christ, the Son of the Living God."

People: We also believe.

Joiner: "I unreservedly and with abandon commit my life and destiny to Christ, promising to give Him a practical priority in all the affairs of life. I will seek first the Kingdom of God and His Righteousness."

People: We join with you in committing our total being to Christ.

Joiner: "I commit myself, regardless of the expenditures of time, energy, and money to becoming an informed, mature Christian."

People: With God's help, we too, make this commitment.

Joiner: "I believe that God is the total owner of my life and resources. I give God the throne in relation to the material aspect of my life. God is the owner. I am the ower. Because God is a lavish giver I too shall be lavish and cheerful in my regular gifts."

People: We rejoice in his goodness.

Joiner: "I will seek to be Christian in all relations with my fellow man, with other nations, groups, classes, and races."

People: With God's help we will so order our lives.

Joiner: "I will seek to bring every phase of my life under the Lordship of Christ."

People: We will work at this with you.

Joiner: "It is my desire and purpose to be baptized in the Christian faith and to be confirmed in the Christian fellowship of the United Methodist Church."

People: We rejoice with you in this decision.

> (*quoted portions from* Call to Commitment, *O'Connor, pp. 20–21*)

CONFIRMATION INTO MEMBERSHIP
(*The people form a circle. The pieces of yarn which had tied them together two by two are attached to the large piece of yarn encircling the room via the long end of yarn left loose.*)

BENEDICTION RESPONSE
"Gloria Patri"

> (Hymns Hot and Carols Cool, *Avery and Marsh, p. 2*)

Reflections

Everything in the service was done in togetherness: In the worship hours itself we tried to point up the corporateness of God's family in two ways—first, in our own verbal participation in readings, songs, and responses to our new member's vows; second, by tying each two persons together at the wrist with a piece of yarn as they entered and later joining these pieces in a large circle. This yarn action symbolized the added strength of the whole community and our openness to others.

In our case we knew before the pastor that one of the early worshipers wished to join our church. When we made the pastor aware of this potential member, we asked his approval of the vows we wished to use, as they are somewhat more incisive than the usual ones. He also shared them with our prospective member well ahead of time.

Group leaders were well informed as to the thrust of the dialogue time so that they could move beyond surface answers into meaningful feelings.

The newer musical settings by Avery and Marsh for the traditional "Praise God from Whom All Blessings Flow" and "Glory Be to the Father" are especially refreshing.

13

Service of Departure

IDEA GERM	We are a family of faith whether together or apart. What better time to emphasize this truth than when a family is leaving our midst.
DESCRIPTION OF SERVICE	A touching service for a family that is moving—not to say good-bye, but to reaffirm the Christian family that is the church. Appropriate songs, readings, and Scripture lead up to the wishes, prayers, and commissions that the congregation offers for the departing family.
PREPARATION CHECKLIST	Arrange for a host family or leader, remembering that this service requires an especially effective reader.

Inform musicians of song selections.

See that bulletins are ready.

Arrange chairs in a circle opening out from the worship center. Allow enough space for the guitars to move freely during the singing.

Assemble pencils, paper, and string.

Service Script: Service of Departure

(As the people enter, each person is given a short piece of string or yarn.)

Leader: This is what will mark the church of Christ as different.

This is what a spiritually starved world will wonder at: "See how they love one another."

Even the hard world of business will take notice. One of our church members recommended another member for an opening in the office of a business acquaintance. Several years later when a new opening came, the same person inquired about placing another member of the church.

"I'm sorry," said the business friend. "I'm not hiring anyone else from your church."

"Why?" she asked, "I thought Peter was working out fine."

"It's not that," he said. "We make it a policy never to hire two people from the same family and your church is too much of a family."

The other day a man in our coffee house asked, "Who runs this place?" and then added, "Let me guess. It's a family."

We are members now of that family of faith with ties deeper than any we have known before.

(from Call to Commitment, O'Connor, *pp. 32–33)*

PRAYER

Leader: Thank God.

Thank God for those who see into us, through us, and to the self that is beyond ourselves. There have been those few who refused our superficial roles, who have seen beyond our clever chatter; who have waited beyond our preoccupation. Reaching through our facades, which we have very carefully built, they have seen a beauty which we all have, but which, for most of us lies buried deep inside. The beauty was planted there by God. He then touches those few, who through love, touch us. Much of the positive which we do and think is in response to those who have smiled past the shell into the white light. Thank God and thank them, and pray we never stop trying to measure up to what he and they believe we can be.

(from God Is No Fool, Cheney, *p. 108)*

SONG SERVICE   "Here We Are"

(Mass for Young Americans, Repp, p. 6)

"In Christ There Is No East or West"

(New Wine: Songs for Celebration,
Strathdee and Stringer, p. 16)

"Magic Penny"

(New Wine: Songs for Celebration, *p. 51*)

"We Are the Church"

(Songs for The Easter People, *Avery and Marsh, p. 20*)

Offering and Concerns

READING

Leader: Bits and Pieces

People. People important to you, people unimportant to you cross your life, touch it with love and carelessness and move on.

There are people who leave you and you breathe a sigh of relief and wonder why you ever came into contact with them. There are people who leave you and you breathe a sigh of remorse and wonder why they had to go away and leave such a gaping hole. Children leave parents; friends leave friends. Acquaintances move on. People change homes. People grow apart. Enemies hate and move on. Friends love and move on. You think on the many who have moved into your hazy memory. You look on those present and wonder.

I believe in God's master plan in lives. He moves people in and out of each other's lives, and each leaves his mark on the other. You find you are made up of bits and pieces of all who ever touched your life, and you are more because of it, and you would be less if they had not touched you.

Pray God that you accept the bits and pieces in humility and wonder, and never question,
and never regret.

(from God Is No Fool, *Cheney, p. 81*)

SCRIPTURE   1 John 4:7–13, 19–21

SERVICE OF SENDING FORTH	*(The leader calls the departing family forward and asks them to answer this question:)*
	"What difference will it make in the world that these people have been together?"
	(The leader then divides the congregation into three groups and asks group 1 to formulate prayers; group 2, wishes; group 3, a commissioning to offer later to their departing friends. Time allotted: ten minutes.)
	(As the groups come back together, the departing family shares first the answer to their question; and then a spokesman for each of the three groups responds with their prayers, wishes, and commissioning.)
FRIENDSHIP CIRCLE	*(The people tie together their short pieces of string to symbolize the family of Christ being strengthened as each member joins. Such a family remains strong no matter where the members are.)*
BENEDICTION	"Peace My Friends"

(Genesis Songbook, *Young, p. 74*)

Reflections

Since we are such mobile people today, worship leaders should be aware of their community members' plans. You may learn of departing families through your church office or via sharing with one another. This service would be as unique as are the departing individuals, even if repeated often.

Should you have more than one family departing at the same time, this service can be adapted to collective use by having each family answer the question posed and by having one group of people to formulate the prayers, wishes, and commissions for each family.

14

A Time to Die

IDEA GERM	To share our sense of loss due to the death of a member of our community and to look a little more closely at death's meanings than we really want to.
DESCRIPTION OF SERVICE	A meaningful adaptation of an experimental funeral liturgy which allows the people to mourn, to search, to face their fears, and to find hope and reassurance.
PREPARATION CHECKLIST	Recruit a dialogue leader.
	Contact a leader for this service.
	Arrange for someone to get records and to play them at the appropriate times.
	Be sure you have someone to run the projector for the film.
	See that the bulletin is prepared.
	Set up room using a center aisle with chairs curved as much as possible to face opposite sides. Don't forget to provide a projector and thread the film through it ahead of time.

Service Script: A Time to Die

MUSICAL INTERLUDE	"Requiem" by Faure

Leader: "No man is an island, entire of itself; every man is a piece of the continent, a part of the main; if a clod be washed away by the sea, Europe is the less, as well as if a promontory were, as well as if a manor of thy friends or of thine own were; any man's death diminishes me, because I am involved in mankind; and therefore never send to know for whom the bell tolls; it tolls for thee."

(*from* Devotions Upon Emergent Occasions, *John Donne*)

Leader: We are saddened.

People: Our grief is great.

Leader: What is the nature of our grief?

People: Death has come to us. We have lost our loved one. We recognize that we will be lonely. Death has come. It is for this that we grieve.

(*"An Experimental Liturgy for the Burial of the Dead" by the Rev. John H. Curtis from* Ventures in Worship 2, *edited by Randolph, p. 186*)

VISUAL
INTERLUDE

For Those Who Mourn

(*from Teleketics Films*)

GOD'S UNDER-
STANDING

Leader: God understands these feelings . . .

"Comfort ye,
Comfort ye, my people,"
says your God.

A voice cries:
In the wilderness prepare the way of the Lord,
Make straight in the desert a highway for our God.
Every valley shall be lifted up
    and every mountain and hill made low,

And the glory of the Lord shall be revealed,
   and all flesh shall see it
   for the Lord has spoken.

A voice says, CRY!
And I said, "What shall I cry?"
All flesh is grass
   and all its beauty like the flowers of
   the field.
The grass withers, the flowers fade
   The grass withers, the flowers fade
But the word of our God will stand forever.
He will feed his flock like a shepherd,
   He will gather the lambs in his arms,
He will carry them in his bosom
   and gently lead those that are with young.

Have you not known? Have you not heard?
   Has it not been told to you from the beginning?
The Lord is everlasting,
   the creator of the ends of the earth.
He does not faint or grow weary.
   His understanding is unsearchable.

He gives the power to the faint
   and to him who has no might he increases strength.
And they who wait upon the Lord
   shall renew their strength.
They shall mount up with wings like eagles,
   They shall run and not be weary,
They shall walk and not faint.

For the Lord, our God reigns
   forever, and ever.
Amen and Amen.

(Based on Isa. 40)

(Adapted from "An Experimental Liturgy for the Burial of the Dead" by Curtis in Ventures in Worship 2, *edited by Randolph, pp. 186–187)*

DIALOGUE ON
DEATH

(Minister shares some thoughts on death and then allows the people to respond or share their own thoughts. Minister concludes dialogue with prayer.)

Leader: These words of comfort lead us beyond grief.

People: Beyond grief? What is beyond grief?

Leader: Faith! For God uses grief to help us realize the potential of our faith. In grieving we find a sense of his strength alive in us. This is new life through the Holy Spirit.

People: Who tells of this Faith? How do we learn of it?

Leader: Our faith is a gift from God. He gives it to us that we might be strong in moments of grief. In this way he bears us up. This faith is an experience that we feel from within. We have learned of it from Jesus who speaks of faith in this life that we might inherit the life which is to come. He speaks of it with these comfortable words:

Let not your hearts be troubled; believe in God, believe also in me. In my Father's house are many rooms; if it were not so, would I have told you that I go to prepare a place for you? And when I go and prepare a place for you, I will come again and will take you to myself, that where I am you may be also.

I am the way, and the truth, and the life; no one comes to the Father but by me. If you had known me, you would have known my Father also.

If you love me you will keep my commandments, and I will pray the Father, and he will give you another Counselor, to be with you for ever, even the Spirit of truth, whom the world cannot receive, because it neither sees him nor knows him; you know him, for he dwells with you, and will be in you.

Peace I leave with you; my peace I give to you; not as the world gives do I give to you. Let not your hearts be troubled, neither let them be afraid.

(John 14:1–4, 6–7, 15–17, 27, RSV)

People: We are no longer afraid. We believe that Jesus does reveal God's will and God's infinite love.

Leader: Love like that of a good shepherd who gathers lambs, who redeems sinners, who grants new life, the life of the Spirit.

People: We believe in new life. We have been born into the life of flesh. That was new life. We have been awakened spiritually. That was new life. We believe in the kingdom. We are told it is a spiritual kingdom. What is it like?

Leader: No man knows. Only Christ has gone before us. Paul's witness in this matter instructs us as he says:

But someone will ask, "How are the dead raised? With what kind of body do they come?" O foolish man! What you sow does not come to life unless it dies. God gives it a body as he has chosen.

So it is with the resurrection of the dead. What is sown is perishable, what is raised is imperishable. It is sown in dishonor, it is raised in glory. It is sown in weakness, it is raised in power. It is sown a physical body, it is raised a spiritual body.

Just as we have borne the image of the physical we shall also bear the image of the spiritual. I tell you this, brethren; flesh and blood does not inherit the Kingdom of God, nor does the perishable inherit the imperishable. For this mortal nature is granted eternal life.

In fact, Christ has been raised from the dead, the first fruits of those who have died. For as by a man came death, now by a man also has come the resurrection of the dead. As in Adam all die, so also in Christ shall all be made alive.

(1 Cor. 15:20–23, 35, 42, 49)

People: We know that we shall all die. We believe that death is not the end. Death is the way we pass from flesh and blood into the Spiritual Kingdom.

Leader: And so in Faith in God's love we face our own ultimate death. You have and are brave. It is not an easy thing to do.

People: We act because we are strengthened by the faith revealed in Jesus Christ, by the love of God for us, and by the hope of life eternal. With this witness we return to the living of the days ahead. . . .

Leader: This is the good news. Take it into your world of daily life and work and make known his love and peace to mankind.

People: May we be blessed by the grace of the Holy Spirit.

Leader: May our Lord Jesus Christ and God our Father fortify in us every good deed and word.

> (adapted from "An Experimental Liturgy for the Burial of the Dead," Curtis, in Ventures in Worship 2, edited by Randolph, pp. 187–190)

SPECIAL MUSIC "How Lovely Is Thy Dwelling Place"

> (from the German Requiem by Brahms)

BENEDICTION

People: The grace of the Lord Jesus Christ, and the love of God, and the fellowship of the Holy Spirit be with us all.

Leader: Amen.

People: Amen.

> (from "An Experimental Liturgy for the Burial of the Dead," Curtis, in Ventures in Worship 2, edited by Randolph, p. 190)

Reflections

The bulk of this worship service was taken from the experimental funeral liturgy found in Ventures in Worship 2. We edited it for our purpose as we mourned the loss of a friend. This service proved to be a moving experience shared together.

In the dialogue on death, we felt that the opportunity for dialogue was appreciated, but not much happened verbally.

15

I'm Lonely, Lord

IDEA GERM
To simulate experiences of loneliness and isolation at a deep feeling level and to explore their meaning for us as individuals living each day.

DESCRIPTION OF SERVICE
Loneliness. Stagnation. Emptiness. Isolation. Soon I exist in a hollow vacuum, not knowing how or why I got here—and more importantly, not knowing how to change. Such a scene is set through darkness, isolation seating, and readings and songs. An expert weaves a fantasy which strengthens my awareness of my own loneliness—unbearably so—and then offers me a wonderful way out!

PREPARATION CHECKLIST
Ask a person who has experience in counseling therapy, dealing with personal and emotional difficulties and personal communications problems, to lead in building a fantasy. This technique is designed to put people in touch with their own loneliness.

Arrange for one or more readers for three readings, the Scripture, and the benediction.

Inform musicians of the song selections. "The Pilgrims Song" should be memorized as the special selection. Remember to tell them that they'll be singing in the dark.

Prepare an order of service and materials for participants. No bulletins, since they cannot be read in the dark.

Place chairs so that no one can touch anyone else—to create the feeling of isolation.

Provide a small flashlight, shielded so that the beam goes to the reading material only. Be sure to have an extra in case of accident. *Note:* The lectern may be placed behind a freestanding screen as an added precaution, taking care that readers can be heard.

See that you have enough candles to use around the room as people enter (if you plan to use them). Candlelight helps people to find seats while retaining the subdued, isolated atmosphere. Have someone extinguish the candles as worship begins and arrange for one or two people to assist latecomers.

Place offering baskets by the exits.

Service Script: I'm Lonely, Lord

READING

I'm not a shoe
tossed in a corner
or an island
lost in the sea,
I'm not an orphan
or an unwanted pet,
but I might as well be,
because I'm alone.

I'm surrounded by people,
but I'm all alone.
Some people laugh with me,
some give advice,
some ask for help
or tell me I'm neat,
but no one seems to stop
and notice who I really am.

I feel so lonely inside
that I've started spinning
a shell to cover myself
and hide
that strange something inside me
that is me.
I don't want to hide it,
but I must.
Otherwise people will see
what I'm really like.

Then they will smile and say:
"What a funny kid."

Tomorrow I'll try to leave my shell . . .
tomorrow, but not today.

I'm surrounded
by friendly people
who seem so happy.
I pretend to be happy.
and warm and comfortable, too.
I don't know what else to do
when I'm with other people.
I'm all alone then. . . .
And yet I can't talk about it
or explain why.
It's like being trapped.

I feel like a withered left hand
hiding behind someone's back.
I'm wearing a glove
to hide myself.
I need my glove,
but I hate it
because it's not really me.
Tomorrow I'll take it off
and exercise my hand . . .
tomorrow, but not today.

I'm so lonely sometimes
I could run away
and just disappear into the air.
But I want those people around me.
I want their love
and their joy in me.
Still they keep slipping past me,
slipping,
slipping away
and never really touching me.
They just see my mask
and slide slowly by.

Tomorrow, Lord, tomorrow,
I'll remove my mask

and people will have to stop
and notice me . . .
tomorrow, when I'm older and stronger
I'll remove my mask . . .
but not today,
please, not today . . .
because today I'm too alone
with so many people around me,
so many people
in this place . . .
a church.

("*Tomorrow, But Not Today,*" Interrobang, *Habel,
pp. 26–27*)

READING

We hurried on, our heads bent against the wind, to the cluster
of lights ahead that was 149th Street and Westchester Avenue,
and those lights seemed to me the brightest lights I had ever
seen. Tugging at my father's coat, I started down the line of
pushcarts. . . . I would merely pause before a pushcart to say,
with as much control as I could muster, "Look at that chemistry set!" or, "There's a stamp album!" or, "Look at the printing press!" Each time my father would pause and ask the
pushcart man the price. Then without a word we would move
on to the next pushcart. Once or twice he would pick up a toy
of some kind and look at it and then at me, as if to suggest this
might be something I might like, but I was ten years old and a
good deal beyond just a toy; my heart was set on a chemistry set
or a printing press. There they were on every pushcart we
stopped at, but the price was always the same and soon I looked
up and saw we were nearing the end of the line. Only two or
three more pushcarts remained. My father looked up, too, and
I heard him jingle some coins in his pocket. In a flash I knew it
all. He'd gotten together about seventy-five cents to buy me a
Christmas present, and he hadn't dared say so in case there was
nothing to be had for so small a sum. As I looked up at him I
saw a look of despair and disappointment in his eyes that
brought me closer to him than I had ever been in my life. I
wanted to throw my arms around him and say, "It doesn't matter. . . . I understand. . . . This is better than a chemistry set or
a printing press. . . . I love you." But instead we stood shivering
beside each other for a moment—then turned away from the
last two pushcarts and started silently back home. . . . I didn't
even take his hand on the way home nor did he take mine. We

were not on that basis. Nor did I ever tell him how close to him I felt that night—that for a little while the concrete wall between father and son had crumbled away and I knew that we were two lonely people struggling to reach each other.

("Two Lonely People" by Moss Hart from Act One)

SILENCE

CONFESSION

> *Leader:* Please respond to our prayer of confession with a word or phrase.
>
> "I'm lonely, Lord, lonely when I _____"

SONG "Jesus Walked This Lonesome Valley"

(Songbook for Saints and Sinners, Young, *p. 24*)

A FANTASY *(Led by an expert.)*

(A fantasy is a story into which one projects himself in order to gain insights or self-understanding. The story is usually begun by a leader with individual participants asked to complete it individually through mental imagery. The group then shares either in subgroups or one to one. It is important to note that interpretation is made only by the person relating his own completion of the fantasy.)

SCRIPTURE Rom. 8:37–39 (TEV)

SONG "The Pilgrims Song"

(Joy Is Like the Rain *collection*)

READING I live where I hear trains. That's good. The night sound of trains surrounds my most quiet and intimate moments. Perhaps each person has a lonely sound with which he has grown up—cars echoing up and down the highway in front of his home; a pine tree murmuring its secrets; a bus laboring, snorting, wheezing its lonely paths; the low mumble of voices in another part of the house. You grow up listening and drifting on the sound. The sound becomes tangled in memories and wonderings and getting older and fears and doubts.

I heard trains as I prayed "Who am I?"

I listened to trains as a loved one left.

I heard trains when life turned into death in a person of my heart.

I hear trains when there is self-doubt.

I hear trains when my mind and imagination drift and wander.

I hear trains when I whisper "Forgive me."

What was the sound in your life? What was it you listened to the sleepless nights as you dreamed beyond your home and family? Where did you spend that night? and what sounds kept you awake that night—that night you ran away from your parents, the night before you spent the day in the temple asking questions? What did you hear after that strange, wild-looking man baptized you? What sounds did you hear when you wandered alone out on the mysterious desert? You liked the sea; was it the lonely wash of water on small beach pebbles you heard? You often climbed hills; was it the sound of wind swirling its lonely stillness? When you crossed the Kidron and spent much of that night in prayer, what lonely earth sound kept you company? High on that cross; when all seemed lost and for nothing; when your lonely cry pierced God's turned back—"Why hast thou forsaken me?"—what did you hear? What did you listen to, those lonely, awful hours?

When I hear trains
And it is quiet
And I am alone
I think of Jesus
And he seems very, very real to me
And it is good when Jesus is real
When he is more than books
  and thoughts
  and hymns
  and prayers
I think I could reach out and touch him.
And I know he can reach out and touch me.

(from God Is No Fool, Cheney, pp. 102–104, #56)

BENEDICTION

Leader: We struggle in separation,
    with silent longing,
      lonely,
      and alone.
    Lord, help us to reach out to each other
      and say "I love you."

(from Creative Brooding, *Raines, p. 47)*

Leader: Reach out now and say "I love you."

Reflections

Darkness is an important ingredient in this service. Our musicians memorized the songs and rehearsed in the dark, yet they had to review the words of "Lonesome Valley" during the song's introduction in the actual worship hour. Our reader's flashlight was dropped as we began, giving us a last-minute scurry. And the room setup was a special one. The effect, however, was quite worth all of the technical arrangements.

Silence is another important ingredient. Don't close it off too soon, as is the tendency. Use short silences along the way, too.

The confession brought responses of single words or phrases from the community and was deeply meaningful.

The person who led the fantasy also called for insights gained. These were shared by the worshiping community at the end of the fantasy meditation time.

Following the benediction reading and the informal words about the risk of loving, came a beautiful moment when our people really did reach out to say "I love you" to someone nearby.

16
Love One Another

IDEA GERM

To examine our commitments to love one another as our Lord commanded.

DESCRIPTION
OF SERVICE

Scripture, poetry, readings, creeds, and songs form the foundation for this service, preparing the people for the highlights—a film and a very moving reading. Then the people stand ready to make the commitment suggested at the end of the service.

PREPARATION
CHECKLIST

Arrange to get the film *A Chairy Tale*.

Contact a leader and readers. Prepare and distribute their parts ahead of time.

A rehearsal for "Look Around You" is desirable, but it can be done with a few minutes of careful explanation prior to the service.

Inform musicians of song selections for their rehearsal.

See that bulletins are created and produced.

Decide how to arrange the room, keeping the film in mind. One way is to use a half-circle with an aisle in the middle, placing the worship center on a low table at center front.

Service Script: Love One Another

THE BEGINNING

Reader: "What? Loving again?"

I asked in dismay.
"And must I keep loving and loving always?"
"Oh, no" said the angel, piercing me through.
"Just love until God stops loving you."

(adapted from Christian Clippings, *November 1972, p. 8)*

SONG   "Oh Brothers Come"

(New Wine: Songs for Celebration,
Strathdee and Stringer, eds., p. 46)

THE SCRIPTURE   Rom. 13:8–10

A NEW CREED

> *Leader:* Let us repeat together a contemporary expression of Christian faith.
>
> Man is not alone, he lives in God's world.
>
> *All:* We believe in God:
>   who has created and is creating,
>   who has come in the true man, Jesus,
>   to reconcile and make new,
>   who works in us and others by his Spirit.
>   We trust him.
>
>   He calls us to be in his Church:
>   to celebrate his presence,
>   to love and serve others,
>   to seek justice and resist evil,
>   to proclaim Jesus, crucified and risen,
>   our judge and hope.
>
>   In life, in death, in life beyond death,
>   God is with us.
>
>   We are not alone.
>
>   Thanks be to God.

(by The United Church of Canada, from Ventures in
Worship 2, *edited by Randolph, p. 92, #63)*

CALL TO CONFESSION	"Create in Me a Clean Heart, O God"
	(New Wine: Songs for Celebration, Strathdee and Stringer, p. 8)

CONFESSION

Leader: God, we find our lives in bondage to things less than Christ-like.

People: Free us from illusions of self-sufficiency and our notions that we do not need you or our neighbors. Free us from the need to always be on the go, from the drive to make our way the right way. Free us for creative and joy filled living.

Leader: Free us from indifference to the needs of human community. From the need to get our own way, to do our own thing, to escape to the mountains, the sea, the highway, or that other place.

People: Release our nation from illusions of innocence and perfection. Free us from idolatry toward country, race, belief, life-style, or ourselves. Free us from reliance on the automobile, the camper, the boat, our home, and all the things we feel we must buy.

Leader: God, direct us into new ways of living; ways that find concern and actions for others central to all that we are and do.

("Seeking to Go Beyond," from Worship Pac, *Issue 17, October 1973, p. 8)*

All: Amen.

OFFERING AND CONCERNS

SONG "Love Them Now"

(Genesis Songbook, *Young, p. 36*)

SCRIPTURE John 15:12–17

PRAYER *(Read silently, then aloud together.)*

All: Give us today, O God, the grace of friendliness, so that we may gladly share the troubles and the joys of those who are in this place with us. Give us the grace to speak the right word, when we speak, and to know when to be silent and to listen to someone else who needs to unburden himself. Help us all in this place and in our homes to come to know each other better today, and so in new friendships to find new strength. But may our friendship with You come above all else. This we ask for Jesus' sake. Amen.

> (Holland-Cypress River Parish, The United Church of Canada, Holland, Manitoba from Worship Pac, Issue 15, July 1973, p. 3)

FILM   "A Chairy Tale" (National Film Board of Canada)

READING

Leader: Look around you, people of God
—Look around you.
Who is the person sitting next to you?

Reader 1: The person next to you is the greatest miracle and the greatest mystery you will ever meet; at this moment a testament of the word made flesh of God's continuing Advent into the world into our midst.

Reader 2: The person next to you is an inexhaustible reservoir of possibility, with potentialities that have been only partially touched.

Reader 3: The person next to you is a unique universe of experience, seething with necessity and possibility, dread and desire, smiles and frowns, laughter and tears, fears and hopes, all struggling to find expression.

Reader 4: The person next to you is surging to become something in particular, to arrive at some destination, to have a story and a song, to be known and to know.

Reader 5: The person next to you believes in something, something precious, stands for something, counts for something, labors for something, waits for something, runs for something, runs toward something.

Reader 6: The person next to you is a whole colony of persons, persons met all during his lifetime, really a community in which still lives a father and mother, a friend and enemy.

Reader 7: The person next to you has some things she can do well; some things she can do better than anyone else in the whole world: there is something her one life on earth means and cares for; but does she dare speak of this to you?

Reader 8: The person next to you can live with you not just alongside; he can live not only for himself, but also for you, he can confront, encounter, understand you, if that is what you want; and in turn, he is to be understood also.

Reader 9: The person next to you can be fully understood; she is more than any description or explanation; she can never be fully controlled, nor should she be.

Leader: The person next to you is mystery—as the word made flesh is mystery.

And the Word was made Flesh and dwelt among us.
So people of God
Look around you.
For God is here!

SONG   "Bridge over Troubled Waters"

(Genesis Songbook, *Young*, *p. 61*)

ACT OF   *(Joined together in a circle)*
COMMITMENT

All: It is only through human relationships, that we discover the living Christ full. For only when we enter into life with Christ can we seek to care and love each other fully.

When we commit ourselves to others in love,
we begin to understand the love of God.
When we grasp the love of God, our response
is to offer our lives to God.

When we give our lives to God, we live for others, placing their needs and concerns above our own.

(from Worship Pac, *Issue 14, May 1973, p. 1)*

BENEDICTION   *(Two leaders demonstrate this person-to-person benediction, and it proceeds naturally around the circle.)*

Giver: ___(name)___ , the peace of Christ is yours.

Receiver: And his love belongs to both of us,___(name)___ .

Reflections

The public library is a source for "A Chairy Tale" and perhaps other films. However, you may need another source which will require advance ordering.

Be sure the readers understand what they are to accomplish in "Look Around You." They should practice their paragraphs at least once or twice. Poor reading can destroy completely the thoughts expressed here which are such good follow-up for the film. Readers should be scattered throughout the congregation for the best effect.

Forming the circle for the act of commitment may present a small technical problem in that bulletins are needed for that section. We joined arms to leave hands free and instructed the worshipers to bring along their bulletins when they formed the circle.

Explicit instructions for the benediction "giving and receiving" are necessary.

17
But if I Have Not Love

IDEA GERM

To examine thoughts and feelings about love or the lack of love. How does our behavior reflect whether we love or not? How can God be the mediator in relationships?

DESCRIPTION
OF SERVICE

A puppet show and the people's reaction to it are highlighted here. A creative opportunity for the puppeteers, and a real treat for the entire congregation.

PREPARATION
CHECKLIST

Recruit a group who will be in charge of the puppet show: selecting or writing a script; making the puppets, stage, and scenery; rehearsing and performing. Allow several weeks (or months) to prepare.

Give musicians a list of song selections. Encourage a rehearsal.

Arrange for a leader—either the pastor or a layman.

Set up the room so that the people have the best possible view of the puppet stage. The traditional theater setup works well.

Have bulletins prepared after consulting the puppeteers.

Service Script: But If I Have Not Love

CALL TO
WORSHIP

Leader: Why are you here?

People:	We have come to worship.
Leader:	Whom do you worship?
People:	We worship the God who created this world and made us in his own image, his children.
Leader:	Why do you worship?
People:	We worship because we recognize that God's wisdom is vastly superior to ours, because we realize that God loves us and wills for his children the best that is possible.
Leader:	Then let us praise this all-wise and everloving Father!

(The Rev. Phil E. Pierce in Ventures in Worship 2, *edited by Randolph, pp. 51–52, #15)*

SONG SERVICE   "Praise Ye the Lord"

(The New Jesus Style Songs, vol. 1, Anderson)

"If I Had a Hammer"

(Genesis Songbook, Young, p. 69)

"Magic Penny"

(New Wine: Songs for Celebration, Strathdee and Stringer, p. 54)

Offering and Prayer

(Leader presides and prays.)

Community Concerns and Interests

SCRIPTURE SHARING   Gal. 6:1–5, 9, 10; Eph. 4:24–27, 32 (TEV)

PRAYER OF CONFESSION   *(Leader should keep service theme in mind when he offers this prayer.)*

ASSURANCE OF PARDON	"Amazing Grace"
	(Genesis Songbook, *Young*, *p. 38*)

PUPPET PRESENTATION	"But If I Have Not Love"

(As a service to your creativity, a puppet script is not included here. A project like this is something out of the ordinary, so jump into it prepared to enjoy some extraordinary results. You'll find books on all aspects of puppets and puppet shows in your library.)

TALK BACK *(Congregation questions the puppet players about show's content. Players' adviser or one of the players presides.)*

BENEDICTION

Leader: What's wrong with me, God?
I hurt my friends
and say rotten things about them.
I brag to them
and use them all like little steps
to make myself feel taller.
I pretend to be concerned
about the things they say,
but what I really want to do
is to enjoy their company
like friendly pets who do not bite.

If I stop and think
about the things I do
I get mad at myself
for being selfish
and stupid and thoughtless.
But tomorrow
I'll probably go out
and do the same things again
without realizing what I do.
Why can't I change?
I know what's wrong
but that doesn't solve anything.

. . . .

If only there were someone
who could stand between us
with a hand on my shoulder
and a hand on yours
to mediate our differences.
Or is that the role
that Jesus Christ, the Jew,
has been waiting centuries
to play for me
and you?

(from "We're Enemies, God," Interrobang,
Habel, pp. 15–16)

People Sing: "Lord I Want To Be More Loving"

(a verse of "Lord, I Want To Be a Christian,"
The Methodist Hymnal, #286, 1964)

Reflections

Since our eighth-grade church school class took on the project
of preparing a puppet show, we planned the rest of the service
around their theme. They decided on the story, wrote the
script, and made puppets, stage, and scenery. However, a group
within your church could prepare a puppet presentation
whether or not you have a theme in mind. Be sure to allow
plenty of time for preparation.

"Talk back" was moderated by the puppeteers' adviser. Members of the worship community took this opportunity to question the young people about the content of the play.

18
Care—Act?

IDEA GERM

To consider the meaning of being God's persons in the world and committing to a real act of caring.

DESCRIPTION OF SERVICE

Scripture, readings, prayers, and songs precede the distribution of MIA (missing in action) bracelets *or other expressions of current concerns.* The people use dialogue groups to consider when they care and how they carry through. After the dialogue is finished, they write letters voicing their concern about our MIAs.

PREPARATION CHECKLIST

Arrange for a host family or a leader.

Notify musicians of song selections.

Have bulletins and lists of questions for the small groups ready. Remember to include necessary information pertaining to current concerns emphasized in your service, e.g., names, addresses, etc.

Use appropriate visual aids.

Have plenty of paper, pens and pencils, and envelopes on hand for the letters.

Remember to stamp and mail the letters after the service.

Service Script: Care—Act?

<table>
<tr><td>CONGREGA-
TIONAL
SINGING</td><td>"If I Had a Hammer"

 (Genesis Songbook, Young, p. 69) </td></tr>
</table>

Greetings and Community Interests

SCRIPTURE   1 Pet. 5:1–7 (TEV)

THOUGHTS FOR
OUR FATHER

Leader: Our Father, who art in heaven . . .

People: Father,
we'd like your undivided attention.
There are some matters we must discuss
with you today.

Leader: Hallowed be thy name . . .

People: It's like this.
Your name is mud in some circles.
People laugh when your name is mentioned.
For some your name is nothing but a cussword.
Restore some honor to your name, Lord.
And help us to do the same.

Leader: Thy kingdom come . . .

People: We have some real difficulties here, Lord.
It's so hard to see your hand at work
in the world around us.
There are so many wars and evils at large.
We want you to take over right now
and to straighten out this mess on earth.
Make this the final takeover.
And use us to do it.

Leader: Thy will be done, on earth as it is in heaven . . .

People: We'd like to point out, Father,
that no one seems to know the plans of heaven
and very few seem to care.
Anyway, your sons are very confused
about what your will is supposed to be on earth.
What kind of change in politics and people
will make this world free and good?
Teach us your plan, put it into operation,
and speed up your timetable.

Leader: Give us this day our daily bread . . .

People: Daily bread is one of our foremost needs.
Millions upon millions are starving.
The world's population is exploding.
How can we use our resources
to develop each man's pride in his own work?
As we tackle this task
give us some of
the rich bread from that banquet table
prepared for men at the end of this age.
We need it now.

Leader: Forgive us our trespasses
as we forgive those who trespass against us . . .

People: We are rather sensitive about this, Father.
We're talking about a chain reaction of forgiving.
That's not so easy. We are proud.
We sometimes feel guilty or miserable
despite your love and acceptance.
And we find it rough trying to forgive some people.
Open our hearts to your love
and give us the power to love others now
as we will in that new age.

Leader: Lead us not into temptation,
but deliver us from evil . . .

People: Father, don't let us have to face
the ultimate test of obedience.
Christ did that for us.

Father, don't let us have to face
the full force of evil.
Christ did that for us.
Father, don't let us have to face death
without you beside us.
Christ did that for us.

Leader: For thine is the kingdom,
and the power,
and the glory,
for ever and ever. Amen.

People: You are God, after all.
You have the power.
You have the plan.
You have the honor.
Take over now and rule forever.
And give us the joy of seeing it happen.
Amen.

Leader: Let it happen, Father.

People: And let it happen now. Amen.

(from Interrobang, Habel, *pp. 87–88)*

CONGREGA-
TIONAL
SINGING

"Blowin' in the Wind"

(Genesis Songbook, *Young, p. 37*)

A NEW CREED

Leader: Let us repeat together a contemporary expression of Christian faith.

Man is not alone, he lives in God's world.

All: We believe in God:
who has created and is creating,
who has come in the true man, Jesus, to reconcile and make new,
who works in us and others by his Spirit.

We trust him.
He calls us to be in his Church:
   to celebrate his presence,
   to love and serve others,
   to seek justice and resist evil,
    to proclaim Jesus, crucified and risen, our judge and our hope.
In life, in death, in life beyond death, God is with us.
We are not alone.

Thanks be to God.

(from Ventures in Worship 2, *edited by Randolph, p. 92)*

DISTRIBUTION OF MIA BRACELETS	*(These bracelets were borrowed from VIVA, but members who wished to keep their bracelets could buy them after the service.)*
PRAYER FOR THE MIAS	*(Each person prays silently for the man whose name is on his bracelet. Then the leader prays aloud.)*

Leader: O God of mercy and compassion assist our men who are missing in action to bear the agony of captivity, speed their return. Inspire those who know to inform the waiting of their loved one's fate. Thy will be done. Amen.

(prayer by Chaplain Richard D'Arcy, Major, U.S. Army, VIVA material)

CARE—ACT? *(The people are divided into small groups to discuss the following:)*

1. Share the times in the past two weeks that you didn't care at all.

2. Share the times in the past two weeks that you thought you cared but did nothing.

3. Share the times in the past two weeks that you cared and then acted on this caring.

FORMULATION OF LETTERS *(After the discussion, each person who is concerned about the MIAs writes a letter to one of the national and international leaders listed in the bulletin.)*

Offering of Gifts and Letters

(Letters, offering, and bracelets taken up simultaneously.)

BENEDICTION
SONG
"I'd Like to Teach the World to Sing"

(Genesis Songbook, *Young, p. 4*)

BENEDICTION
SCRIPTURE

Leader: Do not fool yourselves by just listening to his word. Instead, put it into practice.

People: For whoever listens to the word but does not put it into practice is like a man who looks in a mirror and sees himself as he is.

Leader: He takes a look at himself and then goes away, and at once forgets what he looks like.

People: But the man who looks closely into the perfect law that sets men free, who keeps on paying attention to it, and does not simply listen and then forget it, but puts it into practice—that man will be blessed by God in what he does.

(*James 1:22–25*, TEV)

All: Amen.

Reflections

This particular Sunday was designated as National MIA Awareness Day, sponsored by VIVA (Vital Voices of America). We felt this awareness could be shared appropriately in worship—especially since our worship community is strongly identified with the military community.

VIVA supplied us with MIA bracelets, a prayer, and some visual aids.

Our visual aids included posters of MIAs; red, white, and blue flowers on the worship center table; and hats representing each branch of the service plus a civilian hat on a row of chairs in the front.

This service grew out of the great concern of one of our members for the MIA cause. However, the service could certainly be adapted to any cause. Find out what concerns your members and make this service confirm those concerns.

19

The Gospel Alive

IDEA GERM	To see that we always throw stones in the form of thoughts, words, and actions—just as the people did who threw stones at Stephen.
DESCRIPTION OF SERVICE	The clever use of some rather commonplace visual aids highlight this service that makes us all too aware that stoning is as much a part of today as yesterday.
PREPARATION CHECKLIST	Notify musicians of music to be used. Guitarist or music director should teach new song during preliturgy.

Work out physical expressions for prayer of confession and words of assurance.

Collect stones. They should be fairly small and all shapes.

Arrange for leader, readers, and movement leaders. Readers and movement leaders should have preparation time, practicing together for most effective presentation.

Make use of visual aids on the walls including entry way to setting for worship. Be sure stones are placed near the offering center.

See that bulletins are designed and ready. Be sure to explain the use of movement in the bulletin so your people won't be caught unaware.

Service Script: The Gospel Alive

"When Did We Do It to Thee?"

PRELITURGY

"Create in Me a Clean Heart, O God"

> (New Wine: Songs for Celebration,
> *Strathdee and Stringer, p. 8*)

CALL TO
WORSHIP

Leader: In various ways God spoke of old to our fathers by the prophets.

People: We acknowledge that One who is beyond all times and places and who gives us our life.

Leader: But in these days he has spoken to us by a Son.

People: We received the Word in Jesus Christ as the one redemptive possibility.

Leader: Let us love one another, for love is of God, and he who loves is born of God and knows God.

People: We affirm the call to live our lives as an offering for all mankind.

> (*from* Ventures in Worship 1, *edited by Randolph, p. 11*)

SONG

"Blowing in the Wind"

> (Genesis Songbook, *Young, p. 37*)

SCRIPTURE

Acts 7:54–60

> (The Cotton Patch Version of the Luke and Acts, *Jordan,*
> *gives a refreshing interpretation.*)

PRAYER OF
CONFESSION

People: We are God's people. We live the way of Christ and yet this is how we serve him: We buy guns to make peace in the summer. We ban the books and see the movies. We buy expensive homes and don't increase our pledge. We close the doors of our homes and our minds to those who are different than we are. We destroy cities to save them. We use our age for an excuse for the lack of understanding. We stuff ourselves while others starve. God forgive us!

> *(Hillcrest United Methodist Church, Minneapolis, Minn.,
> in* Ventures in Worship 1, *edited by Randolph, p. 15)*

Leader: As we confess our sins before God, let us give thought to the following: If sin is violent expressions of anger, let us bodily express anger. *(Pause)* If sin is rejection of God's action, let us bodily express rejection. *(Pause)* If sin is selfishness, then let us bodily express selfishness. *(Pause)*

(Two movement leaders flank the leader who reads. As he pauses, these two express their interpretations of anger, rejection, and selfishness.)

WORDS OF
ASSURANCE

Leader: I say to you accept the forgiveness in your hands, *(pause)* head, *(pause)* and heart, *(pause)* which God offers you. You are free of bondage to your past and anxiety in your future.

(The two movement leaders lead interpretations of hands, head, and heart.)

People: We are condemned to be loved by God and to love one another.

> *(adapted, First University United Methodist Church,
> Minneapolis, Minn., from* Ventures in Worship 1, *edited
> by Randolph, p. 25)*

Offering

(The offering is collected, and then the stones on the worship center are passed out to each person.)

People: We present ourselves: our work and our play, our joys and our sorrows, our thoughts and our deeds, just as we are, to be used by God for the sake of all men everywhere.

SONG	"Pass It On"

(from Tell It Like It Is *by Carmichael and Kaiser, p.* 123)

MEDITATION	"Stones"

(Leader talks to the people off-the-cuff about how we throw stones in our daily lives—"everybody does it everyday"—through word, action, and thought.)

SCRIPTURE	John 8:4–9, John 11:8–10 (TEV)
REFLECTION	*(Leader asks the people to think about what he has just said and read and to look at their stones. He pauses and then asks them to share as they feel led.)*
PRAYER	*(Leader begins each segment of prayer pausing for one word or phrase responses.)*

"Lord, forgive us for . . ."
"Lord, thank you for . . ."
"Lord, we accept . . ."
"Lord, we commit . . ."

PRAYER RESPONSE SONG	"Create in Me a Clean Heart, O God"

(New Wine: Songs for Celebration, *Strathdee and Stringer, p.* 8)

BENEDICTION

People: You asked for my hands that You could use
them for Your Purpose.
I gave them for a moment and then withdrew
for the work was hard.

You asked for my mouth to speak out against
injustice.
I gave you a whisper that I might not be
accused.

You asked for my eyes to see the pain of
poverty.
I closed them for I did not want to
know.

You asked for my life that you might work
    through me.
I gave you a fractional part that I might
    not get involved.

Lord, forgive me for calculated efforts to
    serve you only when it is convenient
    to do so,
Only in places where it is safe to do so,
Only with those who make it easy to do so.
Father, forgive me, renew me, and send me out
    as a usable instrument,
That I may take seriously the meaning of
    Your cross.

> ("Renewal," Marilee Zdenek, in Catch the New Wind,
> Zdenek and Champion, p. 121)

Reflections

Our worship community was not ready for the physical expressions of sin in the prayer of confession. Knowing "where they are" is so important. We will try again, since physical expression is a valid method for getting in touch with feelings.

The purpose of distributing stones is to help people understand what stoning is: the stone leaving the hand, the feeling of power, the pain. The connection between the stones and the derogatory words, thoughts, and actions which cause pain for ourselves and others is easily seen.

The reflective meditation pointed out these thoughts and was partly silent.

The one word or phrase prayers were very effective, as our whole community shared them audibly.

20

And He Touched Them

IDEA GERM	To rediscover the importance and value of touch in building relationships through Jesus' example and through some experiences of our own.
DESCRIPTION OF SERVICE	A guest expert in human communications creates the core of this service by searching the Scriptures, explaining the meaning, and leading the group in touch experiences.
PREPARATION CHECKLIST	Look for an expert. We suggest that this is essential! An ordained minister who has specialized in the field of human communications would be ideal. Meet with him to discuss this service—what you think, feel, and hope it will be. Then let him plan, adapt, change the service as he sees fit.

Inform musicians of the song selections.

Arrange chairs in groups of four for easy participation in the word and response to the word.

Have bulletins designed and printed or mimeographed.

Service Script: And He Touched Them

CALL TO WORSHIP	*(Given by leader.)*
HYMN OF PRAISE	"Clap Your Hands"

(New Wine: Songs for Celebration, *Strathdee and Stringer, p. 4*)

Mark 1:40–42, Acts 13:1–3, Matt. 19:13–15 (TEV)

REFLECTIONS
ON THE WORD

Mark 1:40–42   What is your immediate reaction to your touching a leper?

What is the Lord's attitude toward the leper? Name two things Jesus does to show his attitude.

Imagine you are a leper. Why would being touched be significant?

What are some of your earliest memories of being touched or not touched?

See if you can list at least six different meanings of touch and an example of each.

To whom could you minister to by touch this week?

Acts 13:1–3   How were Paul and Barnabus "set apart" for their ministry?

What is the significance of "laying on of hands"? See 1 Tim. 4:14.

For what ministry would God want to set you apart for this week? Be as specific as possible.

Matt. 19:13–15   Imagine you are a child. How would you feel if the Lord Jesus put his arm around you?

What was Jesus demonstrating by this act? Is it for children only? Or does the "child" in all of us need to be held or touched?

Who would you like to hold or touch you? Who would like you to hold or touch them?

COMMENTS ON
TOUCHING
Meaning and Power

(Based on Touching: The Human Significance of Skin, Montague; *and* The Transparent Self, *Journal)*

RESPONSE TO THE WORD	Touch Experiences Reflection on Experiences Offering
	Offering
DOXOLOGY	
COMMISSION-ING TO MINISTRY	
HYMN OF DEDICATION	"They'll Know We Are Christians by Our Love" (New Wine: Songs for Celebration, *Strathdee and Stringer, p. 57*)

Reflections

Our expert based his comments on touching on results of studies done in the area of touch. He contrasted examples of persons who had the benefit of being touched with those who lacked such benefits. He further directed the touch experiences, helped us to reflect on these experiences, and finally commissioned us to a touch ministry. Thus our expert had led us into a truly meaningful and very moving worship.

21

As We Know Each Other, So Do We Know God

IDEA GERM — To focus our thoughts on 1 John 4:18: "God is love and whoever lives in love lives in God and God lives in Him." To think of our failures historically, corporately, personally, and to think of the alternatives as we try to "live in love."

DESCRIPTION OF SERVICE — A film and a series of thought-provoking readings helps this service to focus thoughts on past failures and possible alternatives in God's love.

PREPARATION CHECKLIST — Allow a few weeks to obtain film from the library, a distributor in your area or the company (Teleketics).

Request par... necessary.

Inform the...

See that bul...

Set up the... screen for th... group circles... you have flex...

Use appropri...

Service Script: As We Know Each Other,
So Do We Know God

PRELITURGY   "Love Them Now"

(Genesis Songbook, Young, p. 36)

GREETING

Offering and Community Concerns and Interests

READING

Reader: I do not believe the greatest threat
             to our future
             is from bombs or guided missiles.
             I don't think our civilization will die that way.
             I think it will die when we no longer care.
             Arnold Toynbee has pointed out
             that 19 of 21 civilizations have died from within
             and not by conquest from without.
             There were no bands playing and flags waving
             when these civilizations decayed.
             It happened slowly,
             in the quiet and the dark
             when no one was aware.

("No Bands Played" by Lawrence M. Gould from
In the Stillness Is the Dancing, *Link, p. 100)*

READING

Last night I went to a church service, and during it we sang the old hymn, "What a friend we have in Jesus." I felt strangely embarrassed.

("I Had a Friend," from God Is No Fool, *Cheney, p. 16)*

**PRAYER OF
CONFESSION**

People: Let us admit what we are before God, our failures, our secret desires, our guilt, our hollowness. Let us, with one word or phrase, confess our inability to reveal ourselves to each other.

"God, forgive me for _____."

Leader: God, smash our masks of pretension.

People: And we will express who we really are!

Leader: If we express who we really are, we will find God.

People: In finding ourselves, we find God!

(from First University United Methodist Church, Minneapolis, Minn., in Ventures in Worship 1, *edited by Randolph, p. 15, #14)*

All: Amen.

**OLD
TESTAMENT
LESSON**

Jer. 31:31, 33–34 (RSV)

CREED

All: I hope that I will always be for each man
     what he needs me to be.
I hope that each man's death will diminish me,
     but fear of my own
     will never diminish my joy of life.
I hope that my love for those whom I like
     will never lessen my love
     for those whom I do not.
I hope that another man's love for me
     will never be a measure of my love for him.

I hope that every man will accept me as I am,
 but that I never will.
I hope that I will always ask for forgiveness
 from others,
 but will never need to be asked for my own.
I hope that I will always recognize my limitations,
 but that I will construct none.
I hope that loving will always be my goal,
 but that love will never be my idol.
I hope that every man will always have hope.

("Hope," college student, quoted by Henri J. M. Nouwen, "Intimacy," in In the Stillness Is the Dancing, Link, *p. 62)*

READING

Reader: [God] exists within us
even more intimately
than we exist within ourselves.

His kingdom is within us;
and when he wishes
to show himself,
he chooses a beggar,
a child, a sinner;
and fills that beggar,
that child, that sinner
with love.

Love is his sign.
And by that sign
we shall all know him.

("His Sign" by Louis Evely, "The Gospels Without Myth," in Take Off Your Shoes, Link, *p. 64)*

NEW
TESTAMENT
LESSON

Matt. 25:34–40 (TEV)

VISUAL
SERMON

"Let the Rain Settle It"

(Teleketics Films)

BENEDICTION
SONG
"They'll Know We Are Christians by Our Love"

(New Wine: Songs for Celebration,
Strathdee and Stringer, p. 57)

Reflections

Since the success of this service depends on clear, sensitive
reading, readers practiced until they were comfortable and
could communicate the depth of the reading. To defeat reading
blahs, we changed voices—used more readers and seated them
throughout the congregation so that voices came from different
places.

The preliturgy was a time to learn a new song. The person
leading songs should always be prodding, encouraging, and
working for better participation, so that the full value of the
song is experienced. People are so out of the habit of singing
that leading songs is not always easy.

22

Mute Witness

IDEA GERM

To consider all the puzzles in this world: why this, why that, how could that happen, why am I in this place, what was the purpose? To see that we'll always have questions but that God stands constant as our "absolute."

DESCRIPTION
OF SERVICE

Readings and songs, dealing with the wonders in our world and the fact that through such wonders man finds God, lead up to putting together a giant puzzle—a huge graphic representation of what the reading and singing have been all about.

PREPARATION
CHECKLIST

Contact a leader or a host family.

Tell the musicians the song selections in time for rehearsal.

Have bulletin cover designed and pages printed or mimeographed.

See that a large drawing of Christ is ready. His head should be drawn including features, but his robed body should be only an arms-outstretched outline. This dress and position yields the most space within the figure, while the arms express the idea of Christ in control.

Get people to cut out magazine pictures showing all sides of our contemporary world. These pictures should be fitted into the outline of Christ's figure and backed with construction paper. Finally, the backed pictures should be cut into enough puzzle pieces for each person to have one.

Place the large empty figure of Christ as the focus of the worship center. Use a wall, if possible, because you need a solid surface on which to paste.

Have glue or paste available.

Service Script: Mute Witness

OPENING
READING

Leader: Has not every man,
at one time in his life,
climbed a high hill and surveyed
the quilt of woodlands, fields, and houses
and asked himself: "Why all this?"
Where did it come from? What is it for?

Why the new calf walking with its mother?
Why the fiery sun warming the new plowed fields?
Why the daisies, budding along the fence?
Why this world: being born, growing, dying?
Does it tell me something of the secret
that shadows my own existence?

But hardly before the question forms,
the flower stems and wheat blades point skyward.
But the fiery sun in one corner,
and the endless expanse of blue in the other,
refuse to yield up their secret.
But what they do say
tells me enough.

("*Mute Witness*" *from* In the Stillness Is the Dancing, Link, *p. 61*)

SONGS "Blowin' in the Wind"

(Genesis Songbook, *Young, p. 37*)

"It Was Me"

(*Avery and Marsh*)

GREETINGS

Offering and Community Concerns

A VERSICLE

Leader: If you have the awareness of what you are, you will find God.

People: What does it mean to be?

Leader: He who has a why to live can endure almost anyhow.

People: God breaks in upon me in unexpected ways.

Leader: God makes sense only in terms of our daily lives.

People: But why Jesus?

Leader: His whole life was the cross.

People: The Holy Spirit is the present action of Christ alive.

Leader: The relation between God and people is like a triangle.

People: The Christian must agonize, struggle and act.

Leader: The path to holiness passes through the world of action.

People: The Christian is called to live in the world.

Leader: One way, for modern man.

People: He said "yes" to God.

Leader: We do not ooze into the Kingdom, we choose into it.

People: He who has a why to live can endure almost anyhow.

Leader: The wind blows where it wills.

People: You hear the sound of it, but you do not know whence it comes
or whither it goes.

Leader: So it is with everyone who is born of the Spirit.

People: Born of the Spirit....

(from Princeton United Methodist Church, Princeton, New Jersey, in Ventures in Worship 1, edited by Randolph, p. 41)

SCRIPTURE   Rom. 5:1–5
READING

SONGS   "Amazing Grace"

(Genesis Songbook, Young, p. 38)

            "I Walk the King's Highway"

(New Wine: Songs for Celebration, Strathdee and Stringer, p. 21)

READING

Leader: Cotton candy clouds so fluffy and white,
            Who put you there in a sky of deep blue?
            Or do you just happen to float along
            Pretty and white in the sky so blue?

            Tall mountain, deep valley, fast river, cool stream,
            Show grandeur and majesty in some great scheme.
            All of these wonders that we behold are
            Only a part it cannot be told.

            Master Designer whoever you are,
            All of this beauty both near and afar,
            Can't just have happened. The odds are too great,
            There must be a plan; we're not left to fate.

            All of this beauty is far too convincing,
            Master Designer, your word must be true.
            Of all your creations man is the dearest,
            Help me to simply believe now in you.

("Master Designer" from Tell It Like It Is, Carmichael and Kaiser, p. 34)

PUTTING IT ALL   *(Leader invites people to come up and put the puzzle together.*
TOGETHER   *Pieces are scattered on a nearby table ready for everyone.)*

BENEDICTION
PRAYER

(Given by leader)

BENEDICTION
RESPONSE

Women: Sing for joy to the Lord, all the world!
Worship the Lord gladly, and come before him with joyful
songs!
Never forget that the Lord is God!
He made us, and we belong to him; we are his people, we are
his flock.

(Ps. 100:1–3, Psalms for Modern Man)

Men: May your people worship you as long as the sun shines,
As long as the moon gives light, for all time.
Praise his glorious name forever,
and may his glory fill the whole earth!
Amen! Amen!

(Ps. 72:5, 19, Psalms for Modern Man)

Reflections

"Master Designer" is a musical selection that we used as a spoken text in order to emphasize its meaning.

Putting together our puzzle turned out to be a very rewarding group experience in which we saw Christ strong in the world and the world in him. Several puzzles, however, would probably work better than one. With everyone around one puzzle, we had a space problem.

23

Calling Forth of Gifts

IDEA GERM | To investigate ideas about gifts—our own and those of others. To reexamine the church's role in nurturing its people while they search for themselves in terms of their gifts.

DESCRIPTION OF SERVICE | A film is used as the special vehicle to help the people think about and discuss the utilization of their talents. The film leads into small group discussions, individual reflections, and then total group sharing.

PREPARATION CHECKLIST | Arrange to have the film from either a distribution center or Teleketics Films, if the public library does not have it.

Contact the number of small-group leaders you will need and provide them with the statements listed in the service. All of these statements may be used in each group or divided among the groups according to available time and desired discussion depth.

Ask a worship leader to be in charge of indicated readings and Scripture.

Tell the musicians which songs will be used.

See that the bulletin is ready.

Set up the room, keeping in mind the film and the small group discussion. Have film on projector and ready to roll.

Service Script: Calling Forth of Gifts

GREETING

Leader: I am so glad that you are here, it helps me to realize how beautiful my world is.

(from a poster by M. Rilke)

People: We are glad to be here and to join you in worship.

All: We join together in gladness as we live our faith.

SINGING

"I'm Gonna Sing (Pray, Be, Share) When the Spirit Says Sing"

(Lift Every Voice, p. 41)

"Born Free"

(New Wine: Songs for Celebration, Strathdee and Stringer, p. 35)

"Magic Penny"

(New Wine: Songs for Celebration, p. 54)

INTERESTS AND COMMUNITY CONCERNS

Offering

Leader: It is good to be able to share our gifts.

People: We have many gifts to give: money, talents, self.

All: We give as part of our response to God.

SHARING THE SYMBOLS OF THE CHRISTIAN FAITH

(For several weeks our worship community participated in this project. Aluminum crosses were given to about five members, chosen at random, to carry for our community for one week. The following Sunday each cross-carrier, whether young or old, shared what carrying this symbol had meant.)

| SCRIPTURE | Gen. 3:8–9, Rom. 12:3–5, Matt. 25:14–30 |

FILM   *A Talent for Tony*

(Teleketics Films)

REFLECTIONS
ON THE FILM

SMALL GROUP
DISCUSSION

"The new forms of the Church will be shaped by the need of every man to become the person he can become." (p. 33)

"Or is it possible, that . . . the hour when there rests upon the Church the imperative to find structures for involvement in the world, can also be the hour of finding the inwardness of life, so that in gaining the world the self Christ speaks of is not lost?" (p. 30)

"The outward journey is determined in part by the gifts discovered in the inward journey." (p. 33)

"The discovery of the real self is the way to the treasure hidden in a field. The gift a person brings to another is the gift of himself. Talents are the expression of this self." (p. 38)

"The person who exercises his own gift in freedom can allow the Holy Spirit to do in others what He wants to do" (Gordon Cosby, p. 37)

"The . . . primary mission of the Christian is to call forth the gifts of others. . . . We are to let others know that God is for them and that they can 'be.' 'They can be what in their deepest hearts they know they were intended to be, they can do what they were meant to do.' " (Gordon Cosby, pp. 36–37)

"The person who is having the time of his life doing what he is doing has a way of calling forth the deeps of another. Such a person . . . is not saying the good news. He is the good news." (Gordon Cosby, p. 37)

(thoughts from Journey Inward, Journey Outward, *O'Connor, pp. 30, 33, 36–38)*

INDIVIDUAL
REFLECTIONS

(Pencils and paper are passed out, and the leader asks the people to consider the questions listed in their bulletins. The leader asks the people to take as much time as they need to come up with some real answers—to carry their considerations home if necessary.)

What are my gifts?
Am I using my gifts?
How? For what reason?

TOTAL GROUP
SHARING

(This sharing time is designed primarily for the content of the small groups to be shared; however, some thoughts from individual reflections may come out in the sharing. Individual thoughts should not be probed in this sharing.)

BENEDICTION

Leader: But each of us has been given his gift, his due portion of Christ's bounty . . .
And these were his gifts: some to be apostles, some prophets, some evangelists, some pastors, and teachers, to equip God's people for work in his service, to the building up of the body of Christ. So shall we all at last attain to the unity inherent in our faith and our knowledge of the Son of God—to mature manhood, measured by nothing less than the full stature of Christ.

(Eph. 4:7, 11–13, NEB)

People: We go forth now rejoicing that our gifts can be used by God.

All: Amen.

24

The Giving Tree

IDEA GERM	To celebrate our myriad gifts from God. To focus on the inexpressible gift of his Son as symbolized by the tree.
DESCRIPTION OF SERVICE	A litany and special music set the scene for a very moving and meaningful reading of a beautiful children's book.
PREPARATION CHECKLIST	Find a really good reader to read *The Giving Tree*. Practice is essential.

Arrange for a leader.

Contact a minister to lead the dialogue on the meaning of gifts.

Tell the musicians which song selections to practice. A soloist, ensemble or choir is needed for the special music.

Arrange chairs in a circle with the worship center at the top. Your worship center might consist of a table which holds a large, tree-shaped candelabra, supporting the symbolism used. An empty chair, later occupied by the reader of *The Giving Tree*, should be placed beside the table. Behind it, you might want to hang a large ceiling to floor banner featuring a simple cross and the words, "He Cared Enough to Give the Very Best."

Design and prepare bulletin.

Service Script: The Giving Tree

Leader: We come to praise the Lord.

People: O God, we come recognizing your greatness.

Leader: God, we have been given an abundance of gifts from your love for us.

People: We come today to offer our praise and our thanksgiving, intending to go forth from this place of worship with deeds of love and mercy.

SINGING   "Amazing Grace"

(Genesis Songbook, Young, p. 38)

A LITANY

Leader: Let us rejoice together that not only have we worshiped together, but we have brought the very symbols of our living before Thee.

People: We yearn, we hope, we search for life—and, look, it is here flowing through our times and places. Let us receive and celebrate the gifts of the Lord.

Leader: We give thanks for the universe.

People: It is our home

Leader: for the earth

People: it is the inheritance entrusted into our hands

Leader: for the city of man

People: ours to design and build toward to common good

Leader: for the revolutions which shake our world

People: full of dangers and brand-new potential

Leader: for the power of our technology

People:	with which we can create or destroy
Leader:	for the perplexities which confront us
People:	in which we may discover our tasks
Leader:	for our heritage
People:	which still calls us to the pilgrimage of faith
Leader:	for the visions of our contemporaries
People:	giving us fresh images of our calling
Leader:	we are given the eyes of the spirit
People:	we may discern in the actual ever fresh possibilities of life
Leader:	the promise is everlasting.
Leader:	The gift of the Tree is given . . .
People:	We may see. . . . We may receive. . . . We may love. . . .
All:	Thanks be to God for his inexpressible gift!

> ("A Litany for the World," St. Anthony Park United Methodist Church, St. Paul, Minn., from Ventures in Worship 1, edited by Randolph, p. 44)

SCRIPTURE   John 3:16–17 (TEV)

Concerns and Interests, Offering and Doxology

THE MEANING   *(based on* The Meaning of Gifts *by Tournier)*
OF GIFTS

SPECIAL MUSIC   *(Light the candles.)*

"Into the Woods My Master Went" by Lutkin

(Methodist Hymnal)

READING	The Giving Tree, by *Shel Silverstein*. (Book available through most bookstores.)
	(The reader comes to the worship center and sits in the chair provided to begin the reading.)
SILENT MEDITATION	
BENEDICTION	

Reflections

The dialogue about the meaning of gifts was very fruitful. Even our children wanted to contribute! A good leader here is essential, but many wanted to share feelings about gifts.

As the candles were lighted (perhaps by children) during the special music, our thoughts focused on the tree in the song, heightening our impressions and putting us in touch with the reality of the Crucifixion. The darkness helped to focus attention on the story, and the two candelabras we used gave plenty of light to the reader.

As the reader began the story, we all entered into an extremely moving experience together. This beautiful story points up the enormity of gifts willingly given by the tree, which never stops loving.

25

Let There Be Joy

IDEA GERM	Enthusiasm can be as worshipful as solemnity. Let's praise him in joy—with song, dance, and fellowship.
DESCRIPTION OF SERVICE	This joyous celebration begins with party decorations and singing. The Lord is praised with Scripture, readings, and more singing. Balloon blessings are tapped to everyone. And what better way to cap such a wondrously joyous occasion than by —dancing the Hora!
PREPARATION CHECKLIST	Ask your minister or an enthusiastic layman to tell the "Parable of the Balloon" and to lead in the balloon tapping.

Inform musicians of selections and be sure that they rehearse. Encourage them to show enthusiasm in their music.

Acquire a record of "Hava Nagila" or the sheet music so the musicians can learn to play it for the dancing.

Prepare paper slips for each person with group-identifying words from the song: "I'm Gonna Sing . . ."

Prepare selected thoughts on slips of paper to be distributed at random as the people arrive. Be sure to number these slips so each reader will know when his turn comes.

Select and contact a reader for "It's a Groovy Day, Lord" and the responses to Psalm 150 and 2 Samuel.

Design and produce the bulletins.

Ask a youth group to decorate the room with crepe paper streamers, balloons, posters, etc. Perhaps they will blow up enough balloons for the balloon tapping, too.

Place chairs in a circle around the walls to form a large open space for balloon tapping and dancing.

Ask someone to learn the Hora and to teach it at the end of the service. (This person may prefer to invite some Jewish people to demonstrate and teach this dance.) Perhaps the young people could learn the dance when they decorate and agree to intersperse themselves among the congregation to help teach when the time comes.

Service Script: Let There Be Joy

(The people are given "I'm Gonna Sing [Clap, Jump, Shout, Hug]" slips of paper as they arrive, and they find their group accordingly. Also, the worship leader gives out the selected thoughts to people as they come in and agree to participate. These readers should include all ages and should sit wherever they wish.)

SETTING THE
ATMOSPHERE

(Singing)

"I'm Gonna Sing When the Spirit Says Sing (Clap, Jump, Shout, Hug, Sing)"

(Lift Every Voice, *General Board of Education of the United Methodist Church*)

(Use as a mixer. Each group sings its own verse, and then everyone does everything.)

PRAYER

Leader: It was like a groovy day, Lord: warm bright and no smog. So I took a walk. Only down the street, but a bird sang and some guy was cutting his lawn. And this little kid was eating ice cream, and it was like WOW! Caught a whiff of the flower—lovely. It was a turned-on day, Lord, and I walked into town and the world seemed with it. I saw people and I felt people and I heard people, and I wanted to stretch out my hands and shout: "I love you, I love you!" but I didn't, and neither did they, but it was a groovy day, Lord.

(A Prayer by Rabbi Allen Secher from Catch
the New Wind, *Zdenek and Champion, p. 58*)

SONG	"Here We Are"

(Mass for Young Americans, Repp)

CELEBRATION	"Clap Your Hands"

(New Wine: Songs for Celebration, Strathdee and Stringer, p. 4)

SELECTED THOUGHTS	*(See "Reflections" at the end of this chapter)*

SELECTIONS
FROM LUKE

> *All:* My heart is overflowing with praise of my Lord; my soul is full of joy in God, my Savior.
>
> He has set kings down from their thrones and lifted up the humble.
>
> He has satisfied the hungry with good things, and sent the rich away with empty hands.
>
> Yes, he has helped Israel, his child;
>
> He has remembered the mercy that he promised to our forefathers, to Abraham and his sons for evermore!

(Luke 1:44–47, 52–55, PT)

SONG CELEBRATION	"Praise Ye the Lord, Hallelujah"

(The New Jesus Style Songs, vol. 1, compiled by Anderson)

THE PARABLE OF THE BALLOON

Everyone was happy at the birthday party except one little boy. He had all the usual problems that shy little guys have. He wanted to have fun just like everybody else, but something inside him just always got all tied up. He could never really bring himself to reach out to others, so even the times that should have been the happiest were lonely times for him. He wanted to reach out and be a part of things but he just didn't know how.

One of the other boys picked up a balloon and tapped it to one of his friends. But balloons don't always go where they are tapped. The wind took the balloon on its way until it touched the shoulder of the shy, frightened guy. He didn't know that the balloon wasn't meant for him, and for the first time in his life he felt like he was part of the party, and he really thought that someone had tapped the balloon to him. He took the balloon and with great excitement, he tapped it back. Soon he was playing with the others. A balloon that wasn't really meant for him somehow meant so very much to him.

God's blessings are like that, and we have the power to bring God's blessings to others. Sometimes the blessing we tap to a friend never gets there, and he never knows we sent it, and yet by the wind of the Spirit, God may send our blessings to someone we didn't even know was there.

(from Catch the New Wind, *Zdenek and Champion, p. 63)*

(At this point storyteller leads community in the balloon-tapping experience until all are tapping balloons and sending verbal blessings.)

Offering and Community Concerns

SCRIPTURE

All: Praise the Lord! Praise God in his temple!
 Praise his strength in heaven!
Praise him for the mighty things he has done!
 Praise his supreme greatness!

Praise him with trumpets! Praise him with harps and lyres!
Praise him with drums and dancing!
 Praise him with harps and flutes!
Praise him with cymbals!
 Praise him with loud cymbals!
Praise the Lord, all living creatures!
Praise the Lord!

(Psalm 150, Psalms for Modern Man)

Reader: Can you imagine the Old Testament prophets playing the drums, trumpets and tambourines and shouting praises to God in a worship service?

(from Catch the New Wind, *Zdenek and Champion, p. 47)*

All: And [He] was followed by David and the other leaders of Israel, who were joyously waving branches of juniper trees and playing every sort of musical instrument before the Lord—lyres, harps, tambourines, castanets and cymbals.

And David danced before the Lord with all his might, and was wearing priests' clothing. So Israel brought home the ark of the Lord with much shouting and blowing of trumpets.

(2 *Sam.* 6:5, 14–15, The Living Bible)

Reader: Can you believe, actually *believe* that King David danced up and down the streets when he brought the ark of the Lord into Jerusalem?

(*from* Catch the New Wind, *Zdenek and Champion, p. 47*)

Leader: Let us, with David, dance as we rejoice together in praise of our Lord!

DANCE
CELEBRATION Dance the Hora ("Hava Nagila")

Leader: The Hora is the national dance of Israel, having been brought there from the Balkans. It is danced at many festive occasions to many traditional tunes, and is a symbol of national strength and spirit.

(*Formation: Dancers form a single circle, facing in, without partners. Hands may be joined, or may be extended along neighbors' arms, so elbows or shoulders are gripped.*)

Instructions:
Measure 1. Each dancer steps to the left side with his left foot, and then steps onto his right foot, crossing it behind the left.

Measure 2. The dancer steps to the left side with his left foot. Hopping on the left foot, he swings the right foot across in front of it.

Measure 3. He steps on the right foot in place and then, hopping on it, he swings the left foot across in front of it.

Note: In some versions, the Hora is done to the *right*. Actually, it may be done in either direction, and may have its direction reversed at any time after a brief interlude in which each dancer does this action in place: lightly jump—hold, jump—hold, and jump-jump-jump—hold.

(from Folk Dancing, Kraus, p. 71)

Reflections

The key word for the leaders here is enthusiasm. The minister, song leader, musicians, reader—everyone should be enthusiastic from the start.

We found that a joyful atmosphere was created as people came in and saw the party decorations and were given song and reading words. In addition, rhythm instruments were distributed to be used "as the spirit moved" those who had them.

The reading of the selected thoughts by different voices from different places added to the excitement of the thoughts:

> What if God danced instead of walked?
>
> What if there were no pipe organs in heaven and the angels played guitars, triangles and tambourines?
>
> What if cherubs told jokes and Saint Peter laughed a lot?
>
> What if finger painting were required and heavenly board meetings were held on a merry-go-round where everyone could interrupt?
>
> What else could Easter mean?
>
> What else could all that running from tomb to city with post-funeral picnics by the sea mean, except that God's a holiday in my head and life with Him a party?

(from Words Are No Good if the
Game Is Solitaire, Barks)

Tapping our balloons helped us to know that blessings do not always go where they are directed, since they are all around us and sometimes come from out of the blue.

The Hora is a simple dance, and the music is familiar to almost everyone. Our dancing turned out to be a really marvelous experience.

The ideas for this service were adapted from *Catch the New Wind* by Zdenek and Champion. Since their service is designed for longer than an hour, we found it necessary to adapt it to our limited time structure.

26

Unbutton Your Raincoat
(New Experiences)

IDEA GERM

To open ourselves to new experiences—especially to the new challenge of formulating and coordinating a meaningful worship offering to our Lord.

DESCRIPTION OF SERVICE

A special reading sets the scene as the congregation realizes that they often miss more than they know. To heighten their awareness, they are told, they should try new experiences. Thereafter, they are broken up into small groups, given some materials, and told to plan the worship service. Fifteen minutes later their worship service happens!

PREPARATION CHECKLIST

Arrange for a host family.

Give musicians the preplanned music selections. Inform them that other music may be suggested during the service itself. They should bring along all the song source books—just in case.

Prepare enough numbered slips of paper (numbered 1, 2, 3, 4, or 5) for each person to have one.

Assemble paper, pencils, and Bibles for each group to use.

See that bulletins are ready.

Service Script: Unbutton Your Raincoat

(As the people enter the worship room, each receives a numbered slip of paper and seeks to find others who have the same number. Like numbers sit together.)

PRELITANY   Group Finding

GREETINGS

     Leader: We welcome you in the name of Jesus.

     People: We gather in the name of the Father Almighty.

     Leader: We come opening ourselves to the Holy Spirit, asking him to speak to us, to move us, and to challenge us anew.

     People: Come let us worship together.

SONG   "Joy Is Like the Rain"

                        (Joy Is Like the Rain *collection*)

SPECIAL
READING

     Reader: When I was a Boy Scout,
                 I had a troop leader who . . . would take us
                 on hikes not saying a word,
                 and then challenge us to describe
                 what we had observed: trees, plants,
                 birds, wildlife, everything.
                 Invariably we hadn't seen
                 a quarter as much as he had,
                 not half enough to satisfy him.
                 "Creation is all around you," he would cry,
                 waving his arms in vast inclusive circles.
                 "But you're keeping it out . . .
                 Stop wearing your raincoat in the shower!"

                 I've never forgotten the ludicrous image
                 of a person standing in a shower bath
                 with a raincoat buttoned up to his chin.
                 It was a memorable exhortation
                 to heightened awareness.

                 The best way to discard the raincoat, I've found,
                 is to expose yourself to new experiences.
                 It's routine that dulls the eye and deadens the ear . . .
                 Get rid of that raincoat and let creation in!

                     (*"Unbutton Your Raincoat" by Arthur Gordon in*
                     In the Stillness Is the Dancing, *Link, p. 16*)

SONG	"Seek and Ye Shall Find"	

(New Wine: Songs for Celebration, Strathdee and Stringer, p. 56)

PREPARATION OF THE WORSHIP SERVICE

(The people already are in their groups. Now they are told what each group is to do as the paper, pencils, and Bibles are passed out. Each group is given a list of the worship order. Time allowed for their work is fifteen minutes.)

SHARING IN THE WORSHIP SERVICE	Acts of Praise and Thanksgiving	group 1
	Call to Confession	group 1

Leader:	Let us confess our sins to Almighty God . . .	
	General Confession	group 2
	Offering, Interests and Concerns	group 2
	Offertory Prayer	group 2
	Prayers of Petition and Intercession	group 3
	Scripture Lessons	group 3
	Affirmation of Faith	group 4
	Call to Christian Discipleship	group 5
	Benediction	group 5

III
EPILOGUE

EPILOGUE

Aids to Formulating
Your Own Celebrations

IDEA
GERM #1

Provide art supplies to use in making a visualization of prayers. We used this technique for New Year's prayers, but it could be used for confessional prayers, or intercessory prayers, etc. We then attached our visualizations to a mobile previously hung from the ceiling. Our mobile designer shared some thoughts on balancing the mobile by working together.

IDEA
GERM #2

Develop a service based on scriptural references to Jesus as the light of the world, using many light sources. We used parts of the first ten pages of *Light: A Language of Celebration* by Kent Schneider and Sister Adelaide. Candles, light bulbs, fire, sparklers, flashing lights, an overhead projector, and a slide projector with slides were part of the worship hour. Colored plastic chips in water, patterned plastic trays, glass ashtrays and anything else that light shows through are exciting on the overhead projector.

IDEA
GERM #3

Children's stories often are beautiful sources for worship planning. Consider *Hope for the Flowers* by Trina Paulus or *The Giving Tree* by Shel Silverstein or *Celebrate the Sun* by James Kavanaugh. *The Velveteen Rabbit* by Margery Williams is another possibility.

IDEA
GERM #4

If your pastor has visited the Holy Land, he probably has many pictures or slides. We asked ours to choose slides of the places which had most touched him, the modern man returning to Jesus' historical setting. An effective part of this worship hour can be spent thinking about the historical Jesus and the Jesus ever present with us.

IDEA
GERM #5

During a worship time about love and compassion for others, introduce a list of needs furnished by the family and children's services of your community. See that these needs are specific in nature; whether money, gifts, time, or what—all should be defined. Then ask your worshiping families to consider this list prayerfully throughout the week. At the following service, provide scissors, pencils, and new lists when necessary. Then have your people cut out the need they feel they can meet, write their names and phone numbers on it, and place it in the offering basket with other offerings. Our people approached these needs as families.

IDEA
GERM #6

Provide supplies and ask the people to make slides expressing their thoughts and experiences concerning the Trinity. Place these in a slide projector and show them with a musical background. Such a slide event shows a corporate spectrum of personal feelings, thoughts and experiences with God, the Father; God, the Son; and God, the Holy Spirit. We used this on Trinity Sunday.

IDEA
GERM #7

Use the "stations of the cross" as the base for a meditation and accompany the text with pictures taken around your town, illustrating each of the stations of the cross in contemporary life.

IDEA
GERM #8

Using a theme such as: "Looking Around, How Well Do We See?" or "He Who Has Eyes to See, Let Him See," develop a worship service about the needs for love and service that already exist. We had five persons to share needs in areas such as the social concerns commission of our church, the inner-city ministry, the allied officers group of a local military post, and the community house normally supported by the church.

IDEA
GERM #9

Ask each person in your community to bring a gift-wrapped box containing the gift he would most like to offer to God. His gift can be anything—adoration, need, problems, joy—expressed symbolically as a gift. We placed our gifts in a large basket during a Christmas celebration and later redistributed them at random so that no one got his own gift. Each person unwrapped his gift when he got home, tried to decipher the symbolism and pray for the giver of the gift during the following week.

IDEA
GERM #10

Explore a single idea in a dialogue group by using contemporary records. For example, "He Ain't Heavy, He's My Brother" might be used with a brotherhood theme. Carefully researched recordings can provide several viewpoints for discussion.

IDEA **GERM #11**	One way to express joy in a celebration of life is through greeting cards. Provide materials and let your people create the cards. Then reach out to share your love and joy by sending the people out to place their cards around your town.
IDEA **GERM #12**	Structure a worship hour entitled "Come into His Presence with Singing." This service calls for a really capable song leader, for no word will be spoken. Many songs fit into the various areas of worship: greeting, prayer, confession and pardon, offering, praise, sharing the word, etc. If explanations are needed, the song leader will sing the explanation. Instructions can be printed in the bulletin.
IDEA **GERM #13**	Give the children who are present crayons and paper to use during a dialogue sermon geared for the older congregation. For instance, if the sermon is entitled "The Shapes of Love," ask the children to make a picture of the things they think of when they consider "being loved." These expressions can be mounted and displayed on the wall for a few weeks as a fine contribution to the dialogue.
IDEA **GERM #14**	How about a service designed to help people think about the probable and possible requirements to enter heaven? Supply all kinds of materials: construction paper, pipe cleaners, yarn, paste, plastic and aluminum foil trays and cups, wire, scissors, crayons, and any other items you wish. Split the congregation into small groups and ask each group to design a vehicle which could take them to heaven. Each group then appoints a spokesman to share his group's concept with the entire congregation.
IDEA **GERM #15**	Stretch a long strip of paper along one wall. Provide marking pens and invite people to write any suitable graffiti that comes to mind after meditation upon a given theme. We used this technique after a series of worship services on a single theme having many facets. Such graffiti help people to crystalize and assimilate the input for themselves.
IDEA **GERM #16**	One beautiful celebration experience to try is "The Great Parade" by Avery and Marsh. This service points up the history of the church through its believers, who were strong people of God. (Copies can be ordered from Proclamation Productions, Inc., Orange Square, Port Jervis, New York 12771.) We followed all the instructions given, but continued our parade outside, greeting the people we met and sharing balloons with them as symbols of our joy.

An End to a Beginning

Dear Reader:

We've come to the end of our sharing, but really we've just begun. In our own church we will continue to celebrate, to praise, to worship. We hope that you will begin your celebration by using our services. Use them in all types of settings: a sanctuary, a classroom, a home, out-of-doors—wherever and whenever you want to really celebrate.

Celebrating worship, as you will discover, is much like what happens after you plant and water a seed. Such a seed grows, blooms, withers, dies . . . but only to scatter in order to grow, bloom, wither, and die to scatter again. So, too, in the celebration of Christ in worship, a seed is planted and nurtured until it blooms and brings forth seed to be scattered and planted again. Our celebrations are the seed, the potential, just waiting to be scattered to take root in the life of others who wait expectantly or unknowingly for the growth and the flower of life's fulfillment in Christ.

We invite you to keep in touch wherever you are in this process. Know that we are with you and available to you as we celebrate life in Christ.

Shalom,
Janice and Blair

Bibliography

Anderson, David L. C. *The New Jesus Style Songs*, vol. 1. Minneapolis, Minn.: Augsburg Publishing House, n.d.

Avery, Richard, and Marsh, Donald. *Alive and Singing*. Port Jervis, N.Y.: Proclamation Productions, 1971.

———. *Be Still*. Port Jervis, N.Y.: Proclamation Productions, 1970.

———. *It Was Me*. Port Jervis, N.Y.: Proclamation Productions, 1970.

———. *Songs for the Easter People*. Port Jervis, N.Y.: Proclamation Productions, 1972.

———. *In the Worship Workshop*. Lima, O.: C.S.S. Publishing.

Ayres, Francis O. *The Ministry of the Laity*. Philadelphia, Pa.: Westminster Press, 1962.

Barclay, William. *The Gospel of John*, vols. 1 and 2. Philadelphia, Pa.: Westminster Press, 1956.

Barker, William. *Twelve Who Were Chosen*. Old Tappan, N.J.: Fleming H. Revell, 1957.

Benson, Dennis. *Electric Liturgy*. Richmond, Va.: John Knox Press, 1972.

———, ed. *Recycle*. Pittsburgh, Pa.: Dennis Benson.

Carr, John. *Advent Worship in the Home*. Nashville, Tenn.: Board of Education, United Methodist Church, 1973.

Coleman, Lyman. *Breaking Free*. Waco, Tex.: Creative Resources, Division of Word Books, 1971.

Dessem, Ralph E., ed. *A Guide to Contemporary Worship*. Lima, O.: C.S.S. Publishing, n.d.

Faith at Work editors. *Groups That Work*. Grand Rapids, Mich.: Zondervan, 1964.

Gealy, Fred D. *Celebration*. Nashville, Tenn.: The Graded Press, 1969.

General Board of Education. *Lift Every Voice*. Nashville, Tenn.: United Methodist Church.

Howe, Reuel L. *The Miracle of Dialogue*. New York, N.Y.: Seabury Press, 1963.

Johnson, Ben, ed. *Rebels in the Church*. Waco, Tex.: Word Books, 1970.

Jordan, Clarence. *The Cotton Patch Version of the Luke and Acts: Jesus' Doings and the Happenings*. New York, N.Y.: Association Press, 1969.

Jourard, Sidney M. *The Transparent Self*. New York, N.Y.: Van Nostrand, 1971.

Laymon, Charles M., ed. *The Interpreter's One Volume Commentary on the Bible*. Richmond, Va.: John Knox Press, 1960.

Lemas, Bernard, and Parsons, George. *Litanies for a Space Age*. Lima, O.: C.S.S. Publishing, n.d.

———. "Worship Aids for a Space Age." Lima, O.: C.S.S. Publishing, n.d.

Liturgical Conference. *Liturgy*. A journal.

Ludkin, Jack, and Gluskin, Burrell. *Liturgies of Life*. Lima, O.: C.S.S. Publishing, 1972.

Marshall, Jane. "He Comes to Us as One Unknown." New York, N.Y.: Carl Fischer, 1957.

————. "My Eternal King." New York, N.Y.: Carl Fischer, 1954.

Marshall, Peter. *John Doe, Disciple*. New York, N.Y.: McGraw-Hill. 1963.

Methodist Publishing House. *The Methodist Hymnal*. Nashville, Tenn.: 1964.

Montagu, Ashley. *Touching: The Human Significance of Skin*. New York, N.Y.: Columbia University Press, 1971.

National Jewish Welfare Board for Jewish Personnel in the Armed Services in the United States. *The Passover Haggada*. 1952.

O'Connor, Elizabeth. *Eighth Day of Creation: Gifts and Creativity*. Waco, Tex.: Word Books, 1971.

Phillips, J. B., translator. *The New Testament in Modern English*. New York, N.Y.: Macmillan, 1972–73.

Raines, Robert A. *New Life in the Church*. New York, N.Y.: Harper & Row, 1961.

————. *The Secular Congregation*. New York, N.Y.: Harper & Row, 1968.

Randolph, David J., and Garrett, Bill, eds. *Ventures in Song*. Nashville, Tenn.: Abingdon Press, 1972.

Regelson, Abraham. *Passover Haggada*. Lima, O.: C.S.S. Publishing, 1971.

Reid, Clyde. *Celebrate the Temporary*. New York, N.Y.: Harper & Row, 1972.

Repp, Ray. *Mass for Young Americans*. Los Angeles, Calif.: FEL Church Publications, 1966.

Schneider, Kent, and Adelaide, Sister. *Light: A Language of Celebration*. Chicago, Ill.: The Center for Contemporary Celebration, 1973.

Silverstein, Shel. *The Giving Tree*. New York, N.Y.: Harper & Row, 1964.

Snyder, Ross. *Contemporary Celebration*. Nashville, Tenn.: Abingdon Press, 1971.

Strathdee, Jim, and Stringer, Nelson, eds. *New Wine: Songs for Celebration*. Los Angeles, Calif.: Board of Education, Southern California/Arizona Conference, United Methodist Church, 1969.

Tournier, Paul. *The Meaning of Gifts*. Richmond, Va.: John Knox Press, 1966.

————. *The Meaning of Persons*. New York, N.Y.: Harper & Row, 1957.

Trueblood, Elton. *Company of the Committed*. New York, N.Y.: Harper & Row, 1961.

————. *The Incendiary Fellowship*. New York, N.Y.: Harper & Row, 1967.

VIVA (Vital Voices of America). MIA Posters. Los Angeles, Calif.: VIVA, n.d.

Waits, Jim L. *Advent Worship in the Home*. Nashville, Tenn.: Board of Education, United Methodist Church, 1972.

Westwood Community United Methodist Church. *For Your Meditation on New Year's Eve*. Los Angeles, Calif.: n.d.

White, James. *New Forms of Worship*. Nashville, Tenn.: Abingdon Press, 1971.

Williams, Vaugh. "Hodie." London: Oxford University Press.

Winter, Sister Miriam Theresa. *Joy Is Like the Rain* collection. New York, N.Y.: Vanguard Music.

Young, Carlton R. *The Genesis Songbook*. Carol Stream, Ill.: Agape, 1973.

————. *Songbook for Saints and Sinners*. Carol Stream, Ill.: Agape, 1971.

Records

Audio-Fidelity Records. *Realistic 1971*. Audio-Fidelity Enterprises, Inc.

Avant Garde Records. *Go Tell Everyone*. New York.

Columbia Records. *The German Requiem*, by Johannes Brahms. 1973.

Moore, Ron, and Moore, Bill. *Lo and Behold*. Arthur Smith Recording Studios, Charlotte, N.C.: Martin Recordings.

Mormon Tabernacle Choir, and Philadelphia Symphony. *The Messiah,* by George Frederick Handel. Columbia Masterworks.

Netherlands Chamber Orchestra. *Brandenburg Concertos Nos. 1–6,* by Johann Sebastian Bach. Epic.

Roger Wagner Chorale. *Requiem, Op. 48,* by Gabriel Faure. Capital Records.

Wise, Joseph. "Gonna Sing My Lord." Cincinnati: World Library Publications, 1967.

Word Records. *Lightshine.* Waco, Tex.: n.d.

Films

National Film Board of Canada. *A Chairy Tale.* Distributed by National Film Board, 680 Fifth Avenue, New York, N.Y. 10019.

Teleketics Films. *For Those Who Mourn.* Distributed by Franciscan Communications Center, 1229 South Santee Street, Los Angeles, Calif. 90015.

———. *Let the Rain Settle It.* Distributed by Franciscan Communications Center, 1229 South Santee Street, Los Angeles, Calif. 90015.

———. *A Talent for Tony.* Distributed by Franciscan Communications Center, 1229 South Santee Street, Los Angeles, Calif. 90015.